Leveled Texts
for Social Studies
World Cultures Through Time

SHELL EDUCATION

Reading Level Consultant
Debra J. Housel, M.S.Ed.

English Language Learner Consultant
Marcela von Vacano
Arlington County Schools, Virginia

Gifted Education Consultant
Wendy Conklin, M.A.
Mentis Online
Round Rock, Texas

Special Education Consultant
Dennis Benjamin
Prince William County
Public Schools, Virginia

Contributing Content Authors
Blane Conklin, Ph.D.
Wendy Conklin, M.A.
Christine Dugan, M.A.Ed.
Shirley J. Jordan, M.S.
Gisela Lee, M.A.
Christine Mayfield, M.S.
Kristine M. Quinn, M.S.
Lisa Zamosky

Publisher
Corinne Burton, M.A.Ed.

Associate Editor
Christina Hill, M.A.

Editorial Assistant
Kathryn R. Kiley

Editorial Director
Emily R. Smith, M.A.Ed.

Editor-in-Chief
Sharon Coan, M.S.Ed.

Editorial Manager
Gisela Lee, M.A.

Creative Director
Lee Aucoin

Cover Designer
Neri Garcia

Cover Art
Vova Pomortzeff
Wong Tsu Shi
Jeff Schultes
Shutterstock, Inc.

Imaging
Don Tran
Sandra Riley
Janie Wong

Shell Education

5301 Oceanus Drive
Huntington Beach, CA 92649

http://www.shelleducation.com

ISBN 978-1-4258-0081-9

© 2007 Shell Education

Reprinted 2010

The classroom teacher may reproduce copies of materials in this book for classroom use only. The reproduction of any part for an entire school or school system is strictly prohibited. No part of this publication may be transmitted, stored, or recorded in any form without written permission from the publisher.

Table of Contents

What Is Differentiation?

Over the past few years, classrooms have evolved into diverse pools of learners. Gifted students, English language learners, special needs students, high achievers, underachievers, and average students all come together to learn from one teacher. The teacher is expected to meet their diverse needs in one classroom. It brings back memories of the one-room schoolhouse during early American history. Not too long ago, lessons were designed to be one size fits all. It was thought that students in the same grade level learned in similar ways. Today, we know that viewpoint to be faulty. Students have differing learning styles, come from different cultures, experience a variety of emotions, and have varied interests. For each subject, they also differ in academic readiness. At times, the challenges teachers face can be overwhelming. They struggle to figure out how to create learning environments that address the differences they find in their students.

What is differentiation? Carol Ann Tomlinson at the University of Virginia says, "Differentiation is simply a teacher attending to the learning needs of a particular student or small group of students, rather than teaching a class as though all individuals in it were basically alike" (2000). Differentiation can be done by any teacher who keeps the learners at the forefront of his or her instruction. The effective teacher asks, "What am I going to do to shape instruction to meet the needs of all my learners?" One method or methodology will not reach all students.

Differentiation encompasses what is taught, how it is taught, and the products students create to show what they have learned. When differentiating curriculum, teachers become the organizers of learning opportunities within the classroom environment. These categories are often referred to as content, process, and product.

- **Content:** Differentiating the content means to put more depth into the curriculum through organizing the curriculum concepts and structure of knowledge.

- **Process:** Differentiating the process requires the use of varied instructional techniques and materials to enhance the learning of students.

- **Product:** When products are differentiated, cognitive development and the students' abilities to express themselves improves.

Teachers should differentiate content, process, and product according to students' characteristics. These characteristics include students' readiness, learning styles, and interests.

- **Readiness:** If a learning experience matches closely with students' previous skills and understanding of a topic, they will learn better.

- **Learning styles:** Teachers should create assignments that allow students to complete work according to their personal preferences and styles.

- **Interests:** If a topic sparks excitement in the learners, then students will become involved in learning and better remember what is taught.

4

How to Differentiate Using This Product

The leveled texts in this series help teachers differentiate social studies content for their students. Each book has 15 topics, and each topic has a text written at four different reading levels. (See page 19 for more information.) These texts are written at a variety of reading levels, but all the levels remain strong in presenting the social studies content and vocabulary. Teachers can focus on the same content standard or objective for the whole class, but individual students can access the content at their *instructional* levels rather than at their *frustration* levels.

Determining your students' instructional levels is the first step in the process. It is important to assess their reading abilities often so they do not get tracked into one level. Most upper elementary and secondary teachers have not had much formal training in how to teach or access reading. So, how will you determine the levels at which to present the material to your students? There are a couple of ways you can do this throughout the year.

- **Running records:** While your class is doing independent work, pull your below-grade-level students aside, one at a time. Individually have them read aloud the lowest level of a text (the star level) as you record any errors they make on your own copy of the text. If students read accurately and fluently and comprehend the material, move them up to the next level and repeat the process. You will need to ask comprehension questions to assess their understanding of the material. You can assess their accuracy and fluency by marking the words they say incorrectly and listening for fluent reading. Use your judgment to determine whether students seem frustrated as they read. As a general guideline, students reading below 90% accuracy are likely to feel frustrated as they read. There are a variety of published reading assessment tools that you can use to assess students' reading levels using the running record format.

- **Refer to other resources:** Another way to determine instructional reading levels is to check your students' Individualized Education Plans, ask the school's resource teachers, or review test scores. All of these resources should be able to give you the further information you need to determine at which reading level to begin your students.

Teachers can also use the texts in this series to scaffold the content for their students. At the beginning of the year, students at the lowest reading levels may need focused teacher guidance. As the year progresses, teachers can begin giving students multiple levels of the same text to allow them to work independently to improve their comprehension. This means each student would have a copy of the text at his or her independent reading level and instructional reading level. As students read the instructional-level texts, they can use the lower texts to better understand the difficult vocabulary. By scaffolding the content in this way, teachers can support students as they move up through the reading levels. This will encourage students to work with texts that are closer to the grade level at which they will be tested.

5

General Information About the Student Populations

Below-Grade-Level Students

By Dennis Benjamin

Gone are the days of a separate special education curriculum. Federal government regulations require that special needs students have access to the general education curriculum. For the vast majority of special needs students today, their Individualized Education Plans (IEPs) contain current performance levels but few short-term content objectives. In other words, the special needs students are required to learn the same content objectives as their on-grade-level peers.

Be well aware of the accommodations and modifications written in students' IEPs. Use them in your teaching and assessment so they become routine. If you hold high expectations of success for all of your students, their efforts and performances will rise as well. Remember the root word of *disability* is *ability*. Go to the root of the special needs learner and apply good teaching. The results will astound and please both of you.

English Language Learners

By Marcela von Vacano

Many school districts have chosen the inclusion model to integrate English language learners into mainstream classrooms. This model has its benefits as well as its drawbacks. One benefit is that English language learners may be able to learn from their peers by hearing and using English more frequently. One drawback is that these second-language learners cannot understand academic language and concepts without special instruction. They need sheltered instruction to take the first steps toward mastering English. In an inclusion classroom, the teacher may not have the time or necessary training to provide specialized instruction for these learners.

Acquiring a second language is a lengthy process that integrates listening, speaking, reading, and writing. Students who are newcomers to the English language are not able to process information until they have mastered a certain number of structures and vocabulary words. Students may learn social language in one or two years. However, academic language takes up to eight years for most students.

Teaching academic language requires good planning and effective implementation. Pacing, or the rate at which information is presented, is another important component in this process. English language learners need to hear the same word in context several times, and they need to practice structures to internalize the words. Reviewing and summarizing what was taught are absolutely necessary for English language learners.

General Information About the Student Populations *(cont.)*

English Language Learners *(cont.)*

Oral language proficiency is the first step in the language learning process. Oral language is defined as speaking and listening skills. English language learners are able to attain word level skills (decoding, word recognition, and spelling) regardless of their oral language proficiency. However, an English language learner's ability to comprehend text and to develop writing skills is dependent on his or her oral language proficiency. Therefore, "vocabulary knowledge, listening comprehension, syntactic skills and the ability to handle meta-linguistic aspects of language, such as being able to provide the definitions of words, are linked to English reading and writing proficiency" (August and Shanahan 2006). First language oral proficiency also has an impact on developmental patterns in second language speech discrimination and production, intra-word segmentation, and vocabulary.

On-Grade-Level Students

By Wendy Conklin

Often, on-grade-level students get overlooked when planning curriculum. More emphasis is usually placed on those who struggle and, at times, on those who excel. Teachers spend time teaching basic skills and even go below grade level to ensure that all students are up to speed. While this is a noble thing and is necessary at times, in the midst of it all, the on-grade-level students can get lost in the shuffle. We must not forget that differentiated strategies are good for the on-grade-level students, too. Providing activities that are too challenging can frustrate these students, and on the other hand, assignments that are too easy can be boring and a waste of their time. The key to reaching this population successfully is to find just the right level of activities and questions while keeping a keen eye on their diverse learning styles.

There are many ways to differentiate for this population. Strategies can include designing activities based on the Multiple Intelligence theory. Current brain research points to the success of active learning strategies. These strategies provoke strong positive emotions and use movement during the learning process to help students learn more effectively. On-grade-level students also benefit from direct teaching of higher-level thinking skills. Keep the activities open-ended so that these students can surprise you with all they know. The strategies described on pages 9–17 were specifically chosen because they are very effective for meeting the needs of on-grade-level students as well as special populations.

General Information About the Student Populations *(cont.)*

Above-Grade-Level Students

By Wendy Conklin

In recent years, many state and school district budgets have cut funding that has in the past provided resources for their gifted and talented programs. The push and focus of schools nationwide is proficiency. It is important that students have the basic skills to read fluently, solve math problems, and grasp science concepts. As a result, funding has been redistributed in hopes of improving test scores on state and national standardized tests. In many cases, the attention has focused only on improving low test scores to the detriment of the gifted students who need to be challenged.

Differentiating through the products you require from your students is a very effective and fairly easy way to meet the needs of gifted students. Actually, this simple change to your assignments will benefit all levels of students in your classroom. While some students are strong verbally, others express themselves better through nonlinguistic representation. After reading the texts in this book, students can express their comprehension through different means, such as drawings, plays, songs, skits, or videos. It is important to identify and address different learning styles. By assigning more open-ended assignments, you allow for more creativity and diversity in your classroom. These differentiated products can easily be aligned with content standards. To assess these standards, use differentiated rubrics.

All students should be learning, growing, and expanding their knowledge in school. This includes gifted students, too. But they will not grow and learn unless someone challenges them with appropriate curriculum. Doing this can be overwhelming at times, even for the experienced teacher. However, there are some strategies that teachers can use to challenge the gifted population. These strategies include open-ended questions, student-directed learning, and using tiered assignments. (See pages 16–17 for more information about each of these strategies.)

Strategies for Using the Leveled Texts

Below-Grade-Level Students

By Dennis Benjamin

KWL Chart

Too often, below-grade-level students fall prey to low expectations. In some classrooms, below-grade-level students even buy into this negative mentality. They begin to reply "I don't know" when they are asked any question. The **KWL** strategy empowers students to take back ownership over their learning. This strategy can be used as a prereading strategy with the texts in this book. **K** stands for *What I Know*. This first part of the process allows students to access prior knowledge and begin to make connections to the new learning about to take place. For example, when asked what they **K**now about ancient Egypt, students will reply with responses such as pyramids, mummies, pharaohs, and the Nile River.

The astute teacher praises the special needs students for how much they know about ancient Egypt and challenges them with the *What Do You **Want** to Know?* column. Encourage the students to create meaningful questions that cannot be answered with simply yes or no. Initially the teacher may model the questions, but ultimately students need to generate their own questions such as: *Why did the Egyptians build pyramids?* and *How big were the pyramids?* Now, the students have set a purpose for reading nonfiction. The reading is no longer about what the teacher wants or expects. Inquisitive minds have been opened to discover what the texts have to offer.

The **L** is for *What I **Learned***. After reading, the students should get back into a group to complete this third column. Students should then record the answers to the questions they wrote and any important concepts they learned from the text. Some students may benefit from identifying the source of information by writing such terms as *text*, *classroom talk*, or *homework* after each entry. That way, they can remember from where their answers came. Take the time to correct any misconceptions.

Once completed, it is important for the teacher to validate students' responses as they review the KWL chart. Praise the students for all the effort they put into the chart and highlight that they, as the learners, were responsible for its completeness and accuracy. This final step is important to help empower your below-grade-level students and encourage them to care more about their own learning.

Strategies for Using the Leveled Texts (cont.)

Below-Grade-Level Students (cont.)

Vocabulary Scavenger Hunt

Another prereading strategy is a Vocabulary Scavenger Hunt. Students preview the text and highlight unknown words. Students then write the words on specially divided pages. The pages are divided into quarters with the following headings: *Definition*, *Sentence*, *Examples*, and *Nonexamples*. A section called *Picture* is put over the middle of the chart.

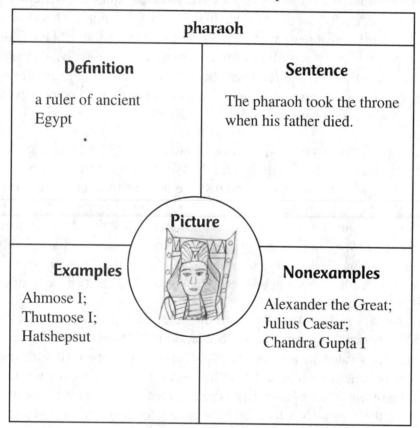

pharaoh	
Definition a ruler of ancient Egypt	**Sentence** The pharaoh took the throne when his father died.
Examples Ahmose I; Thutmose I; Hatshepsut	**Nonexamples** Alexander the Great; Julius Caesar; Chandra Gupta I

This encounter with new vocabulary enables students to use it properly. The definition identifies the word's meaning in student friendly language. The sentence should be written so that the word is used in context. This helps the student make connections with background knowledge. Illustrating the sentence gives a visual clue. Examples help students prepare for factual questions from the teacher or on standardized assessments. Nonexamples help students prepare for **not** and **except for** test questions such as "All of the following are pharaohs *except for . . .*" and "Which of these people is *not* a pharaoh?" Any information the student was unable to record before reading can be added after reading the text.

Strategies for Using the Leveled Texts (cont.)

Below-Grade-Level Students (cont.)

Graphic Organizers to Find Similarities and Differences

Setting a purpose for reading content focuses the learner. One purpose for reading can be to identify similarities and differences. This is a skill that must be directly taught, modeled, and applied. The authors of *Classroom Instruction That Works* state that identifying similarities and differences "might be considered the core of all learning" (Marzano, Pickering, and Pollock 2001, 14). Higher-level tasks include comparing and classifying information and using metaphors and analogies. One way to scaffold these skills is through the use of graphic organizers, which help students focus on the essential information and organize their thoughts.

Example Classifying Graphic Organizer

Ancient civilizations	Location	Gods	Famous leader	End of civilization
Mayas	Mesoamerica	gods of nature		remains a mystery
Aztecs	Mesoamerica	Quetzalcoatl	Moctezuma	Spanish took control
Incas	South America	gods of lightning, thunder, mountains, sun	Sapa Inca/ Atahualpa	Spanish took control

The Riddles Graphic Organizer allows students to compare and contrast ancient civilizations using riddles. Students first complete a chart you've designed. Then, using that chart, they can write summary sentences. They do this by using the riddle clues and reading across the chart. Students can also read down the chart and write summary sentences. With the chart below, students could write the following sentences: *The Mayas and Aztecs lived in Mesoamerica. The Incas and Aztecs lost to Spanish control.*

Example Riddles Graphic Organizer

Who are we?	Mayas	Incas	Aztecs
Our civilization ended when the Spanish took control.		x	x
Our civilization is located in Mesoamerica.	x		x
Our leader is called the Sapa Inca.		x	
Our civilization is located in South America.		x	
Our god is named Quetzalcoatl.			x

Strategies for Using the Leveled Texts (cont.)

Below-Grade-Level Students (cont.)

Framed Outline

This is an underused technique that bears great results. Many below-grade-level students have problems with reading comprehension. They need a framework to help them attack the text and gain confidence in comprehending the material. Once students gain confidence and learn how to locate factual information, the teacher can fade out this technique.

There are two steps to successfully using this technique. First, the teacher writes cloze sentences. Second, the students complete the cloze activity and write summary sentences.

Example Framed Outline

The Middle East was hot and dry. There was lots of _____. But, a place called the _____ Crescent had rich _____ for farming. Ancient _____ was located in the Fertile Crescent. Each year, the two _____ flooded the land. When the water went down, it left a new layer of _____. This soil was good for growing _____.

Summary sentences: *Ancient Mesopotamia was located in the Fertile Crescent. This place had good soil for farming because of the flooding of the two rivers.*

Modeling Written Responses

A frequent criticism heard by educators is that below-grade-level students write poor responses to content-area questions. This problem can be remedied if resource and classroom teachers model what good answers look like. While this may seem like common sense, few teachers take the time to do this. They just assume all children know how to respond in writing.

So, this is a technique you may want to use before asking your students to respond to the comprehension questions associated with the leveled texts in this series. First, read the question aloud. Then, write the question on an overhead and talk aloud about how you would go about answering the question. Next, write the answer using a complete sentence that accurately answers the question. Repeat the procedure for several questions so that students make the connection that quality written responses are your expectation.

As a warm-up activity, post a variety of responses to a single question. Ask students to identify the strongest responses and tell why they are strong. Have students identify the weakest answers and tell why they are weak. Ask for volunteers to come to the overhead and rewrite the weak responses so that they are strong. By doing this simple process, you are helping students evaluate and strengthen their own written responses.

Strategies for Using the Leveled Texts *(cont.)*

English Language Learners

By Marcela von Vacano

Effective teaching for English language learners requires effective planning. In order to achieve success, teachers need to understand and use a conceptual framework to help them plan lessons and units. There are six major components to any framework. Each is described in more detail below.

1. **Select and Define Concepts and Language Objectives**—Before having students read one of the texts in this book, the teacher must first choose a social studies concept and language objective (reading, writing, listening, or speaking) appropriate for the grade level. Then, the next step is to clearly define the concept to be taught. This requires knowledge of the subject matter, alignment with local and state objectives, and careful formulation of a statement that defines the concept. This concept represents the overarching idea. The social studies concept should be written on a piece of paper and posted in a visible place in the classroom.

   By the definition of the concept, post a set of key language objectives. Based on the content and language objectives, select essential vocabulary from the text. The number of new words selected should be based on students' English language levels. Post these words on a word wall that may be arranged alphabetically or by themes.

2. **Build Background Knowledge**—Some English language learners may have a lot of knowledge in their native language, while others may have little or no knowledge. The teacher will want to build the background knowledge of the students using different strategies such as the following:

   Visuals—Use posters, photographs, postcards, newspapers, magazines, drawings, and video clips of the topic you are presenting. The texts in this series include multiple primary sources for your use.

   Realia—Bring real-life objects to the classroom. If you are teaching about ancient Egypt, bring in items such as maps of the pyramids, linen to represent mummification, and examples of hieroglyphics.

   Vocabulary and Word Wall—Introduce key vocabulary in context. Create families of words. Have students draw pictures that illustrate the words and write sentences about the words. Also be sure you have posted the words on a word wall in your classroom.

   Desk Dictionaries—Have students create their own desk dictionaries using index cards. On one side, they should draw a picture of the word. On the opposite side, they should write the word in their own language and in English.

13

Strategies for Using the Leveled Texts *(cont.)*

English Language Learners *(cont.)*

3. **Teach Concepts and Language Objectives**—The teacher must present content and language objectives clearly. He or she must engage students using a hook and must pace the delivery of instruction, taking into consideration the students' English language levels. The concept or concepts to be taught must be stated clearly. Use the first languages of the students whenever possible or assign other students who speak the same languages to mentor and to work cooperatively with the English language learners.

   Lev Semenovich Vygotsky, a Russian psychologist, wrote about the Zone of Proximal Development (ZPD). This theory states that good instruction must fill the gap that exists between the present knowledge of a child and the child's potential. Scaffolding instruction is an important component when planning and teaching lessons. English language learners cannot jump stages of language and content development. You must determine where the students are in the learning process and teach to the next level using several small steps to get to the desired outcome. With the leveled texts in this series and periodic assessment of students' language levels, teachers can support students as they climb the academic ladder.

4. **Practice Concepts and Language Objectives**—English language learners need to practice what they learn with engaging activities. Most people retain knowledge best after applying what they learn to their own lives. This is definitely true for English language learners. Students can apply content and language knowledge by creating projects, stories, skits, poems, or artifacts that show what they learned. Some activities should be geared to the right side of the brain, like those listed above. For students who are left-brain dominant, activities such as defining words and concepts, using graphic organizers, and explaining procedures should be developed. The following teaching strategies are effective in helping students practice both language and content:

   Simulations—Students recreate history by becoming a part of it. They have to make decisions as if they lived in historical times. For example, students can pretend that they are archaeologists, preparing to excavate an Egyptian tomb. They have to figure out what tools they will need to pack and what historical items they hope to discover. First, they need to brainstorm ideas. Then, they present their findings to the class and give explanations for why they chose each tool and how it will help them on their excavation.

Strategies for Using the Leveled Texts (cont.)

English Language Learners (cont.)

4. Practice Concepts and Language Objectives (cont.)

Literature response—Read a text from this book. Have students choose two people described or introduced in the text. Ask students to create a conversation the people might have. Or, you can have students write journal entries about events in the daily lives of the historic people.

Have a short debate—Make a controversial statement such as, "*The Roman senators were justified in killing Julius Caesar.*" After reading a text in this book, have students think about the question and take a position. As students present their ideas, one student can act as a moderator.

Interview—Students may interview a family member or a neighbor in order to obtain information regarding a topic from the texts in this book. For example: *Has any ancient civilization influenced your life today?*

5. Evaluation and Alternative Assessments—We know that evaluation is used to inform instruction. Students must have the opportunity to show their understanding of concepts in different ways and not only through standard assessments. Use both formative and summative assessment to ensure that you are effectively meeting your content and language objectives. Formative assessment is used to plan effective lessons for a particular group of students. Summative assessment is used to find out how much the students have learned. Other alternative assessments that show day-to-day progress are: text retelling, teacher rating scales, students' self-evaluations, cloze testing, holistic scoring of writing samples, performance assessments, and portfolios. Periodically assessing student learning will help you ensure that students continue to receive the correct levels of texts.

6. Home-School Connection—The home-school connection is an important component in the learning process for English language learners. Parents are the first teachers, and they establish expectations for their children. These expectations help shape the behavior of their children. By asking parents to be active participants in the education of their children, students get a double dose of support and encouragement. As a result, families become partners in the education of their children and chances for success in your classroom increase.

You can send home copies of the texts in this series for parents to read with their children. You can even send multiple levels to meet the needs of your second language parents as well as your students. In this way, you are sharing your social studies content standards with your whole second language community.

Strategies for Using the Leleveled Texts (cont.)

Above-Grade-Level Students

By Wendy Conklin

Open-Ended Questions and Activities

Teachers need to be aware of activities that provide a ceiling that is too low for gifted students. When given activities like this, gifted students become bored. We know these students can do more, but how much more? Offering open-ended questions and activities will give high-ability students the opportunities to perform at or above their ability levels. For example, ask students to evaluate major events described in the texts, such as: "Do you agree with Gandhi's method of nonviolent protest?" or "What do you think of the caste system in India?" These questions require students to form opinions, think deeply about the issues, and form pro and con statements in their minds. To questions like this, there really is not one right answer.

The generic, open-ended question stems listed below can be adapted to any topic. There is one leveled comprehension question for each text in this book. The question stems below can be used to develop further comprehension questions for the leveled texts.

- In what ways did . . .
- How might you have done this differently . . .
- What if . . .
- What are some possible explanations for . . .
- How does this affect . . .
- Explain several reasons why . . .
- What problems does this create . . .
- Describe the ways . . .
- What is the best . . .
- What is the worst . . .
- What is the likelihood . . .
- Predict the outcome . . .
- Form a hypothesis . . .
- What are three ways to classify . . .
- Support your reason . . .
- Compare this to modern times . . .
- Make a plan for . . .
- Propose a solution . . .
- What is an alternative to . . .

Strategies for Using the Leveled Texts *(cont.)*

Above-Grade-Level Students *(cont.)*

Student-Directed Learning

Because they are academically advanced, above-grade-level students are often the leaders in classrooms. They are more self-sufficient learners, too. As a result, there are some student-directed strategies that teachers can employ successfully with these students. Remember to use the texts in this book as jumpstarts so that students will be interested in finding out more about the time periods. Your above-grade-level students may enjoy any of the following activities:

- Writing their own questions, exchanging their questions with others, and grading the responses.
- Reviewing the lesson and teaching the topic to another group of students.
- Reading other nonfiction texts about this time period to further expand their knowledge.
- Writing the quizzes and tests to go along with the text.
- Creating illustrated time lines to be displayed as visuals for the entire class.
- Putting together multimedia presentations using primary sources from the time period.
- Leading discussion groups about the texts or time periods.
- Researching topics from the texts and writing new texts on these topics.

Tiered Assignments

Teachers can differentiate lessons by using tiered assignments, or scaffolded lessons. Tiered assignments are parallel tasks designed to have varied levels of depth, complexity, and abstractness. All students work toward one goal, concept, or outcome, but the lesson is tiered to allow for different levels of readiness and performance levels. As students work, they build on their prior knowledge and understanding. Students are motivated to be successful according to their own readiness and learning preferences.

Guidelines for writing tiered lessons include the following:

1. Pick the skill, concept, or generalization that needs to be learned.
2. Think of an on-grade-level activity that teaches this skill, concept, or generalization.
3. Assess the students using classroom discussions, quizzes, tests, or journal entries and place them in groups.
4. Take another look at the activity from Step 2. Modify this activity to meet the needs of the below-grade-level and above-grade-level learners in the class. Add complexity and depth for the above-grade-level students. Add vocabulary support and concrete examples for the below-grade-level students.

How to Use This Product

Readability Chart

Title of the Text	Star	Circle	Square	Triangle
Mesopotamia and the Fertile Crescent	1.9	3.1	5.1	6.7
More Mesopotamian Empires	2.0	3.2	4.7	6.5
Ancient Egypt	2.1	3.3	5.2	6.8
Rulers of Egypt	2.1	3.3	5.0	7.2
Ancient Greece	2.0	3.0	5.1	6.5
Greek City-States	2.2	3.2	5.0	6.8
The Mighty Roman Empire	2.2	3.0	5.0	6.6
The Rise and Fall of the Roman Empire	2.2	3.1	5.0	7.1
Early India	2.1	3.0	4.5	6.5
Indian Rulers	2.2	3.2	5.0	6.9
Ancient China	1.9	3.2	5.0	6.7
More Chinese History	2.2	3.1	5.1	6.5
African History	2.2	3.3	5.0	6.5
Mesoamerican Empires	2.0	3.2	5.0	6.5
The Incredible Incas	2.1	3.0	5.0	6.5

Correlation to Standards

The No Child Left Behind (NCLB) legislation mandates that all states adopt academic standards that identify the skills students will learn in kindergarten through grade 12. While many states had already adopted academic standards prior to NCLB, the legislation set requirements to ensure the standards were detailed and comprehensive. In many states today, teachers are required to demonstrate how their lessons meet state standards. State standards are used in the development of Shell Education products, so educators can be assured that they meet the academic requirements of each state.

Shell Education is committed to producing educational materials that are research and standards based. In this effort, all products are correlated to the academic standards of the 50 states, the District of Columbia, and the Department of Defense Dependent Schools. A correlation report customized for your state can be printed directly from the following website: **http://www.shelleducation.com**. If you require assistance in printing correlation reports, please contact Customer Service at 1-877-777-3450.

McREL Compendium

Shell Education uses the Mid-continent Research for Education and Learning (McREL) Compendium to create standards correlations. Each year, McREL analyzes state standards and revises the compendium. By following this procedure, they are able to produce a general compilation of national standards. The social studies standards on which the texts in this book focus are correlated to state standards at **http://www.shelleducation.com**.

18

How to Use This Product *(cont.)*

Components of the Product

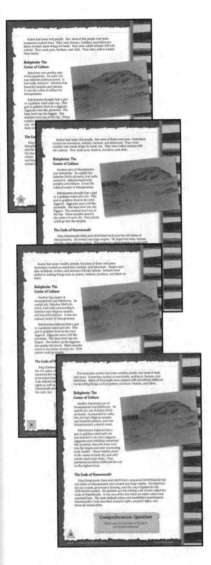

Primary Sources

- Each level of text includes multiple primary sources. These documents, photographs, and illustrations add interest to the texts. The historical images also serve as visual support for English language learners. They make the texts more context rich and bring the texts to life.

Comprehension Questions

- Each level of text includes one comprehension question. Like the texts, the comprehension questions were leveled by an expert. They are written to allow all students to be successful within a whole-class discussion. The questions for the same topic are closely linked so that the teacher can ask a question on that topic and all students will be able to answer. The lowest-level students might focus on the facts, while the upper-level students can delve deeper into the meanings.

- Teachers may want to base their whole-class question on the square level questions. Those were the starting points for all the other leveled questions.

The Levels

- There are 15 topics in this book. Each topic is leveled to four different reading levels. The images and fonts used for each level within a topic look the same.

- Behind each page number, you'll see a shape. These shapes indicate the reading levels of each piece so that you can make sure students are working with the correct texts. The reading levels fall into the ranges indicated to the left. See the chart on page 18 for specific levels of each text.

Levels
1.5–2.2

Levels
3.0–3.5

Levels
4.5–5.2

Levels
6.5–7.2

Leveling Process

- The texts in this series are taken from the *Primary Source Readers* kits published by Teacher Created Materials. A reading expert went through the texts and leveled each one to create four distinct reading levels.

- After that, a special education expert and an English language learner expert carefully reviewed the lowest two levels and suggested changes that would help their students comprehend the texts better.

- The texts were then leveled one final time to ensure the editorial changes made during the process kept them within the ranges described to the left.

How to Use This Product (cont.)

Tips for Managing the Product

How to Prepare the Texts

- When you copy these texts, be sure you set your copier to copy photographs. Run a few test pages and adjust the contrast as necessary. If you want the students to be able to appreciate the images, you need to carefully prepare the texts for them.

- You also have full-color versions of the texts provided in PDF form on the CD. (See page 144 for more information.) Depending on how many copies you need to make, printing the full-color versions and copying those might work best for you.

- Keep in mind that you should copy two-sided to two-sided if you pull the pages out of the book. The shapes behind the page numbers will help you keep the pages organized as you prepare them.

Distributing the Texts

- Some teachers wonder about how to hand the texts out within one classroom. They worry that students will feel insulted if they do not get the same papers as their neighbors. The first step in dealing with these texts is to set up your classroom as a place where all students learn at their individual instructional levels. Making this clear as a fact of life in your classroom is key. Otherwise, the students may constantly ask about why their work is different. You do not need to get into the technicalities of the reading levels. Just state it as a fact that every student will not be working on the same assignment every day. If you do this, then passing out the varied levels is not a problem. Just pass them to the correct students as you circle the room.

- If you would rather not have students openly aware of the differences in the texts, you can try these ways to pass out the materials.

  - Make a pile in your hands from star to triangle. Put your finger between the circle and square levels. As you approach each student, you pull from the top (star), above your finger (circle), below your finger (square), or the bottom (triangle). If you do not hesitate too much in front of each desk, the students will probably not notice.

  - Begin the class period with an opening activity. Put the texts in different places around the room. As students work quietly, circulate and direct students to the right locations for retrieving the texts you want them to use.

  - Organize the texts in small piles by seating arrangement so that when you arrive at a group of desks you have just the levels you need.

Mesopotamia and the Fertile Crescent

Ancient Mesopotamia was located in the Middle East. This land was surrounded by the Tigris (TIE-gruhs) and Euphrates (you-FRAY-teez) rivers. Today, four countries are located there. They are Turkey, Syria (SEAR-ee-uh), Iran, and Iraq.

The Middle East was hot and dry. There was lots of sand. But, a place called the Fertile Crescent (FUHR-tuhl KRES-uhnt) had rich soil for farming. Mesopotamia was located in the Fertile Crescent. Each year, the two rivers flooded the land. When the water went down, it left a new layer of soil. This soil was good for growing crops.

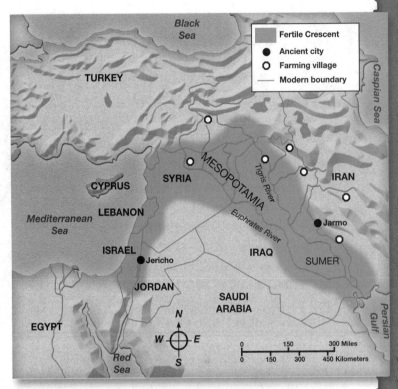

Many people lived in the Fertile Crescent. They lived near the rivers. The people had water for themselves, their animals, and their crops. They could use boats to go places and trade goods.

Sumer: The Cradle of Civilization

People lived in Mesopotamia 7,000 years ago. Sumer (SUE-muhr) was one of its first cities. Sumer ruled itself as a city-state. It was a trade center. Goods were bought, sold, and traded there.

The Sumerians (sue-MER-ee-uhnz) had a form of writing. At first they used pictures. Then, their writing changed. They used symbols called cuneiform (kyou-NEE-uh-form). These symbols were pressed into wet clay. Only a few men could write. These men were called scribes. Scribes were important people. A boy had to go to school for 12 years to become a scribe.

21

Sumer had some rich people. But, most of the people were poor. Sumerians worked hard. They were farmers, builders, and fishermen. Many workers made things by hand. They were called artisans (AR-tuh-zuhnz). They made pots, baskets, and cloth. Then, they sold or traded these items.

Babylonia: The Center of Culture

Babylonia was another part of Mesopotamia. Its main city was Babylon (BAB-uh-lawn). It had walls around it. Babylon had beautiful temples and palaces. It was the center of culture for Mesopotamia.

Babylonians thought that a god or a goddess ruled each city. This god or goddess lived in a ziggurat. Ziggurats were like pyramids. The base level was the biggest. The smallest level was at the top. These temples stood in the center of each city. Only priests could go into these temples.

The Code of Hammurabi

King Hammurabi (ham-muh-RAW-bee) ruled the city-states of Mesopotamia. He formed one big empire. He improved taxes, houses, and the way crops got water. This is called irrigation (ir-ruh-GAY-shuhn). He also wrote laws called the Code of Hammurabi. The code listed crimes. It gave a punishment for each crime. It told how to get loans and how to pay back the money. Hammurabi told people how to treat women and the poor, too.

Comprehension Question

Name one reason that people lived near the rivers.

#50083 — *Leveled Texts: World Cultures*

Mesopotamia and the Fertile Crescent

Ancient Mesopotamia was in the Middle East. It was located on the land surrounding the Tigris (TIE-gruhs) and Euphrates (you-FRAY-teez) rivers. Now, the countries of Turkey, Syria (SEAR-ee-uh), Iran, and Iraq are located there.

Most of the Middle East had a hot, dry climate. But an area called the Fertile Crescent (FUHR-tuhl KRES-uhnt) had rich soil for farming. The Fertile Crescent included Mesopotamia. Each year, the Tigris and Euphrates rivers flooded. When the water went down, there was a new layer of soil to grow crops.

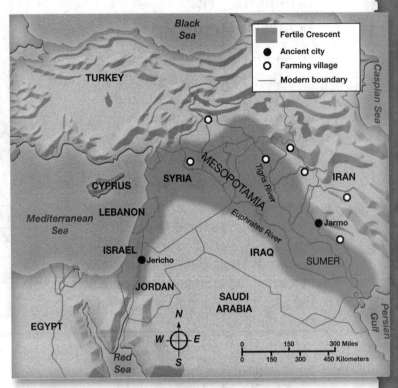

Many people came to the Fertile Crescent. They liked living near the water. The rivers let the people easily get water for themselves, their animals, and their crops. They could use boats to travel and trade goods.

Sumer: The Cradle of Civilization

People lived in Mesopotamia 7,000 years ago. One of its first cities was Sumer (SUE-muhr). As a city-state, Sumer ruled itself. Many goods were bought and sold there. It was a trade center.

The Sumerians (sue-MER-ee-uhnz) had a form of writing. At first they used pictures. Soon their writing changed. They used cuneiform (kyou-NEE-uh-form), or symbols. These marks were made with a pointed stick on wet clay tablets. The stick was called a stylus (STY-luhs). Just a few men called scribes could write. Scribes were important. Some boys went to school for 12 years to become scribes.

Sumer had some rich people. But most of them were poor. Sumerians worked as merchants, builders, farmers, and fishermen. There were workers who made things by hand, too. They were called artisans (AR-tuh-zuhnz). They made pots, baskets, furniture, and cloth.

Babylonia: The Center of Culture

Another part of Mesopotamia was Babylonia. Its capital city, Babylon (BAB-uh-lawn), had walls around it. Babylon had lovely temples and palaces. It was the cultural center of Mesopotamia.

Babylonians thought that a god or a goddess ruled each city. This god or goddess lived in the city's ziggurat. Ziggurats were a bit like pyramids. The base level was the biggest. The smallest level was at the top. These temples stood in the center of each city. Only priests could go into the temples.

The Code of Hammurabi

King Hammurabi (ham-muh-RAW-bee) took over the city-states of Mesopotamia. He formed one large empire. He improved taxes, houses, and the crop-watering system. This system is called irrigation (ir-ruh-GAY-shuhn). He also wrote laws called the Code of Hammurabi. The code defined crimes and their punishments. It covered owners' rights and how to get loans and pay back debts. Hammurabi told people how to treat women and the poor in his code, too.

Comprehension Question

How did the rivers affect life in the Fertile Crescent?

24

Mesopotamia and the Fertile Crescent

Ancient Mesopotamia was in the Middle East. It was located on the land surrounding the Tigris (TIE-gruhs) and Euphrates (you-FRAY-teez) rivers. Today, the countries of Turkey, Syria (SEAR-ee-uh), Iran, and Iraq are located there.

Most of the Middle East had a hot, dry climate. However, an area known as the Fertile Crescent (FUHR-tuhl KRES-uhnt) had rich soil that grew good crops. The Fertile Crescent included Mesopotamia. Each year the Tigris and Euphrates rivers flooded. After each flood, there was a new layer of silt ideal for farming.

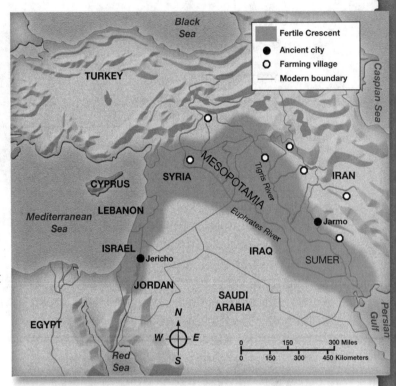

Many people came to the Fertile Crescent because they liked living near the water. The rivers let the people easily get water for themselves, their animals, and their crops. They could also travel and trade goods by using boats on the rivers.

Sumer: The Cradle of Civilization

People lived in Mesopotamia 7,000 years ago. One of its first cities was Sumer (SUE-muhr). As a city-state, Sumer ruled itself. Since so many goods were bought and sold there, it became a trade center.

The Sumerians (sue-MER-ee-uhnz) had a form of writing. At first they wrote using pictures. Soon, their writing developed into cuneiform (kyou-NEE-uh-form), a set of complex symbols. These marks were made on wet clay tablets with a stylus (STY-luhs). Only a few important men called scribes could write. They were respected. Some boys attended special schools for 12 years to become scribes.

25

Sumer had some wealthy people, but most of them were poor. Sumerians worked as merchants, farmers, and fishermen. People were also architects, scribes, and artisans (AR-tuh-zuhnz). Artisans were skilled at making things such as pottery, baskets, furniture, and fabric by hand.

Babylonia: The Center of Culture

Another big empire in Mesopotamia was Babylonia. Its capital city, Babylon (BAB-uh-lawn), had walls surrounding it. Babylon had religious temples and beautiful palaces. It was the cultural center of Mesopotamia.

Babylonians believed that a god or a goddess ruled each city. This god or goddess lived in the city's ziggurat. Ziggurats were a bit like pyramids. The base level was the largest. The further up the ziggurat, the smaller the levels. These temples stood in the center of each city. Only priests could go inside.

The Code of Hammurabi

King Hammurabi (ham-muh-RAW-bee) conquered (KAHN-kuhrd) the city-states of Mesopotamia and created one large empire. He improved the crop irrigation (ir-ruh-GAY-shuhn) system, tax system, and government housing. He wrote laws called the Code of Hammurabi. The code defined crimes and set forth punishments. It described property rights as well as how to get loans, make deposits, and repay debts. Hammurabi described women's rights and the treatment of the poor in his code, too.

Comprehension Question

For what reasons did people want to live in the Fertile Crescent?

26

Mesopotamia and the Fertile Crescent

Ancient Mesopotamia was a large area in the Middle East surrounding the Tigris (TIE-gruhs) and Euphrates (you-FRAY-teez) rivers. Today, the countries of Turkey, Syria (SEAR-ee-uh), Iran, and Iraq are located there.

Most of the Middle East had a hot, dry climate and sandy soil. However, an area called the Fertile Crescent (FUHR-tuhl KRES-uhnt) had rich soil that grew good crops. The Fertile Crescent included Mesopotamia. Every year the Tigris and Euphrates rivers flooded, and after the waters receded, the area had a new layer of silt ideal for farming.

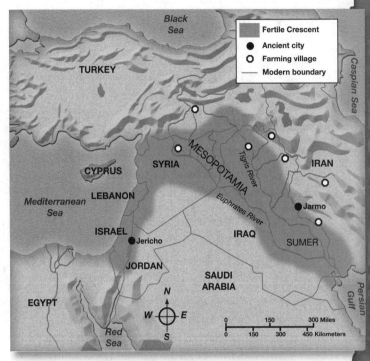

Many people came to live in the Fertile Crescent. The people could easily obtain water from the rivers for themselves, their animals, and their crops. They could also use the rivers to travel and transport goods.

Sumer: The Cradle of Civilization

People lived in Mesopotamia 7,000 years ago. One of its earliest cities was Sumer (SUE-muhr). As a city-state, Sumer ruled itself. Since so many products were bought and sold there, it became a trade center.

The Sumerians (sue-MER-ee-uhnz) developed a form of writing. At first they wrote using simple pictures, but soon their writing developed into cuneiform (kyou-NEE-uh-form). Cuneiform was complex symbols made on wet clay tablets with a stylus (STY-luhs). Only a few highly respected and important men called scribes could read and write. Boys attended special schools for 12 years to become scribes.

27

The Sumerian society had some wealthy people, but most of them were poor. Sumerians worked as merchants, architects, farmers, and fishermen. Many of the people were artisans (AR-tuh-zuhnz) skilled at handcrafting things such as pottery, furniture, baskets, and fabric.

Babylonia: The Center of Culture

Another important part of Mesopotamia was Babylonia. Its capital city was Babylon (BAB-uh-lawn). Surrounded by walls, this city had religious temples and beautiful palaces, and was Mesopotamia's cultural center.

Babylonians believed that a god or goddess ruled each city and dwelled in the city's ziggurat. Ziggurats were buildings somewhat like pyramids since the base level was the largest and each succeeding level was smaller. These temples stood in the center of each city, and only priests could enter them. They performed sacrifices (SAK-ruh-fice-ez) on the highest level.

The Code of Hammurabi

King Hammurabi (ham-muh-RAW-bee) conquered (KAHN-kuhrd) the city-states of Mesopotamia and created one large empire. He improved the tax system, government housing, and the crop irrigation (ir-ruh-GAY-shuhn) system. His greatest act was writing a set of laws called the Code of Hammurabi. It was one of the first times an entire nation had standard laws. The code defined crimes and established punishments. Hammurabi's Code described women's rights, property rights, and financial transactions.

Comprehension Question

What were the benefits of living in the Fertile Crescent?

28

More Mesopotamian Empires

Ancient empires ended a long time ago. Still, they changed the world. The Assyrians (uh-SEAR-ee-uhnz) learned how to do math. The Phoenicians (fih-NEE-shuhnz) found out how to navigate (nav-uh-GAYT). This means they knew where they were at sea. The Hebrews wrote. Their writings form the basis for three faiths. They are Judaism, Christianity, and Islam.

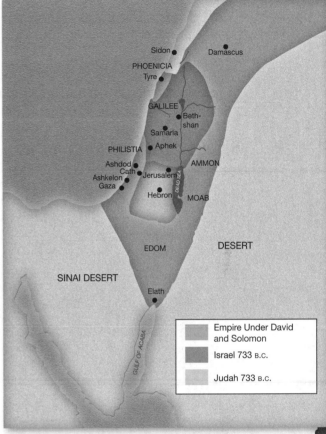

The Hebrews and Their God

The Hebrews lived near the Mediterranean (MED-uh-tuhr-RAY-nee-uhn) Sea. They were between Egypt and Assyria. They worked as shepherds, farmers, and fishermen.

Religion was important to them. The Hebrews believed in one God. They wanted to obey his rules. They wrote the first five books of the Bible. One book tells of a time when there was not much food. This is called a famine (FAM-uhn). Crops failed. Many hungry Hebrews went to Egypt. They went to buy food. But, the Egyptian (ee-JIP-shun) pharaoh (FAIR-oh) got upset. He was the ruler of Egypt. He thought that the Hebrews would take over. So, he made the Hebrews his slaves. After many years, these slaves fled from Egypt.

Tolerant Persians

The Persian (PURR-zhuhn) Empire was the biggest empire in Mesopotamia. It went from Egypt to India. When the Persian Empire won wars, they let the people who lost keep their faith. They did not make them change religions.

Cyrus (SY-ruhs) the Great was a Persian king. Cyrus took over Babylonia. Yet he did not destroy the city of Babylon (BAB-uh-lawn). He was kind to the people. He did not want to ruin their culture. Cyrus even fixed Babylon's temples.

29

Nebuchadrezzar II (neb-yuh-kuh-DREZ-zuhr the second), a Babylonian king, was not kind. He had made the Hebrews his slaves. In 539 B.C., Cyrus let them go home. They went to Jerusalem. Cyrus rebuilt the Hebrew temple there.

Fierce Assyrian Fighters

Assyria was a strong empire in Mesopotamia. The Assyrian king was head of the army. Many of the men were soldiers. Others were farmers or merchants. They were also musicians and scribes. Scribes were the only men who could read and write.

The Assyrians were fighters. They spent years at war. They always wanted more land. When they won, they were not kind to those who had lost.

ʼaleph	[ʼ]		lamedh	[l]
beth	[b]		mem	[m]
gimel	[g]		nun	[n]
daleth	[d]		samekh	[s]
he	[h]		ʼayin	[ʼ]
waw	[w]		pe	[p]
zayin	[z]		tsade	[s]
heth	[h]		qoph	[q]
teth	[t]		resh	[r]
yodh	[y]		shin	[sh]
caph	[k]		taw	[t]

Talented Phoenicians

The Phoenicians had the first alphabet. They made the first blown glass. They made purple dye. They used it to dye cloth. Purple cloth was rare. It cost a lot. Only royalty could buy it.

The Phoenicians built wooden ships. Wood was rare in this dry place. Yet, the Phoenicians had forests. Many people wanted to take their land.

Their culture peaked around 1000 B.C. They sailed to Italy, Africa, and Spain. They traded with people in these nations. But in 576 B.C., the Assyrians took over. Phoenician culture ended.

Comprehension Question

Choose one empire and explain how it influences life today.

30

More Mesopotamian Empires

Ancient empires existed long ago. Yet, they did things that changed the world. The Assyrians (uh-SEAR-ee-uhnz) figured out things about math. The Phoenicians (fih-NEE-shuhnz) used navigation. This means that they could tell where they were at sea. The Hebrews wrote about religion. Their writings form the basis for three major faiths. They are Judaism, Christianity, and Islam.

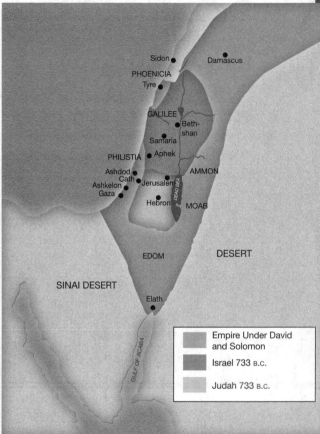

The Hebrews and Their God

The Hebrews lived on the edge of Mesopotamia. They were between Egypt and Assyria on the Mediterranean (MED-uh-tuhr-RAY-nee-uhn) Sea. They worked as shepherds, farmers, and fishermen.

Religion was important to the Hebrews. They believed in one God. They wanted to obey his rules. Their story is told in the first five books of the Bible. It tells of a time when there was not much food. This is called a famine (FAM-uhn). Crops failed. The hungry Hebrews went to Egypt. They wanted to buy food. So many Hebrews came that the Egyptian (ee-JIP-shun) pharaoh (FAIR-oh) got upset. He was the ruler of Egypt. He feared that the Hebrews would take over. To keep control, he made the Hebrews his slaves. After many years, these slaves fled from Egypt.

Tolerant Persians

The Persian (PURR-zhuhn) Empire was the biggest empire in Mesopotamia from 539–330 B.C. It reached from Egypt to India. When the Persians won wars, they let the people who lost keep their faith. They did not force them to change religions.

Cyrus (SY-ruhs) the Great was a Persian king. Cyrus took over many lands, including Babylonia. Yet he promised not to ruin the city of Babylon (BAB-uh-lawn). He showed respect for their religion and culture. Cyrus even fixed Babylon's temples.

31

Nebuchadrezzar II (neb-yuh-kuh-DREZ-zuhr the second), a Babylonian king, was not kind. He had made the Hebrews his slaves. In 539 B.C., Cyrus let the Hebrews go home. They went to Jerusalem. Cyrus also rebuilt the Hebrew temple there.

Fierce Assyrian Fighters

Assyria was a strong empire in Mesopotamia. As in other city-states, the Assyrian king was head of the army. Many of the men were soldiers. Others were farmers or merchants. They were also moneylenders, poets, musicians, and scribes. Scribes were the only men who could read and write.

The Assyrians were fighters. They spent years fighting for more land. When they won, they were not kind to those who had lost.

	'aleph	[']		lamedh	[l]
	beth	[b]		mem	[m]
	gimel	[g]		nun	[n]
	daleth	[d]		samekh	[s]
	he	[h]		'ayin	[']
	waw	[w]		pe	[p]
	zayin	[z]		tsade	[s]
	heth	[h]		qoph	[q]
	teth	[t]		resh	[r]
	yodh	[y]		shin	[sh]
	caph	[k]		taw	[t]

Talented Phoenicians

The Phoenicians had the first alphabet. They made the first blown glass. They made purple dye from snails, too. They used it to dye cloth. Purple cloth was rare. It cost so much that only royalty could afford to wear it.

The Phoenicians built wooden ships. Wood was rare in this dry area. The Phoenicians had cedar and pine forests. Many people wanted to take their land.

Their culture peaked around 1000 B.C. That's when they traded with Italy, Africa, and Spain. But in 576 B.C., the Assyrians took over. The Phoenician culture ended.

Comprehension Question

Choose two empires and explain how they influence life today.

32

More Mesopotamian Empires

Ancient civilizations (siv-uh-luh-ZAY-shuhnz) existed thousands of years ago. Yet, they still influence our lives today. The Assyrians (uh-SEAR-ee-uhnz) improved mathematical knowledge. The Phoenicians (fih-NEE-shuhnz) used navigation. This means that they could tell where they were at sea. The Hebrews' writings form the basis for three major religions. They are Judaism, Christianity, and Islam.

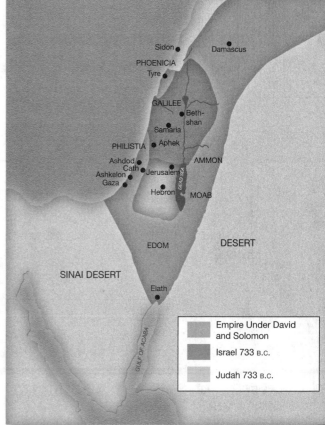

The Hebrews and Their God

The Hebrews lived on the edge of Mesopotamia between Egypt and Assyria on the Mediterranean (MED-uh-tuhr-RAY-nee-uhn) Sea. They were shepherds, farmers, and fishermen.

Religion was important to the Hebrews. Their religion was different from others in Mesopotamia. They believed in one God. They said that God had chosen them, and they had to obey his rules. The Hebrews' story is told in the first five books of the Bible. There was a great famine (FAM-uhn), and the crops failed. Hebrews went to Egypt to get food. So many Hebrews came into Egypt that the Egyptian (ee-JIP-shun) pharaoh (FAIR-oh) began to worry they would take over. He was the ruler of Egypt. To keep control, he made the Hebrews slaves. After many years, they escaped from Egypt.

Tolerant Persians

The Persian (PURR-zhuhn) Empire was the largest in Mesopotamia from 539–330 B.C. It stretched from Egypt to India. One of its greatest kings was Cyrus (SY-ruhs) the Great. He brought together the kingdoms of Medes and Persia. Cyrus took over many lands, including Babylonia. He promised not to ruin the city of Babylon (BAB-uh-lawn). He respected their religion and culture. When the Persians took over, they let the people keep their religions. Cyrus even fixed Babylon's temples.

33

Nebuchadrezzar II (neb-yuh-kuh-DREZ-zuhr), a Babylonian ruler, had taken the Hebrews as slaves. In 539 B.C., Cyrus allowed the Hebrews to return to Jerusalem. Cyrus also rebuilt the Hebrew temple there.

Fierce Assyrian Fighters

Assyria was a strong empire in Mesopotamia. The Assyrians were fierce warriors. They spent years battling for control of more land. They wanted to enlarge the Assyrian Empire. They treated the people that they conquered (KAHN-kuhrd) poorly.

Like other empires and city-states, the king was head of the army. Many Assyrian men were soldiers. Others were farmers or merchants. They were also moneylenders, poets, musicians, and scribes. Scribes were the only men who knew how to read and write.

✶	'aleph	[']	ᗡ	lamedh	[l]
⟩	beth	[b]	⟨	mem	[m]
⟍	gimel	[g]	ᚱ	nun	[n]
◁	daleth	[d]	⧧	samekh	[s]
⟃	he	[h]	○	'ayin	[']
Y	waw	[w]	⟲	pe	[p]
I	zayin	[z]	⟋	tsade	[s]
⊟	heth	[h]	⟟	qoph	[q]
⊗	teth	[t]	⟃	resh	[r]
⟋	yodh	[y]	W	shin	[sh]
⟋	caph	[k]	X	taw	[t]

Talented Phoenicians

The Phoenicians lived in the Middle East. They built wooden ships. Wood was rare and highly prized in this region, and the Phoenicians had cedar and pine forests. Many people wanted to take their land.

The Phoenicians had the first alphabet. They were the first to make blown glass. They knew how to make purple dye from a certain snail, too. They used it to dye fabric. Royalty wore purple because it was rare and costly.

Their culture peaked around 1000 B.C. At that time, they traded with Italy, Africa, and Spain. In 576 B.C., the Assyrians took over, and the Phoenician culture declined.

Comprehension Question

Explain at least three ways that these empires influence life today.

#50083— *Leveled Texts: World Cultures*   © *Shell Education*

More Mesopotamian Empires

Although ancient civilizations (siv-uh-luh-ZAY-shuhnz) existed thousands of years ago, they still influence our lives. The Hebrews created writings that form the basis for the religions of Judaism, Christianity, and Islam. The Assyrians (uh-SEAR-ee-uhnz) increased mathematical knowledge. The Phoenicians (fih-NEE-shuhnz) developed the first alphabet and used navigation to sail the seas. This meant that they could tell where they were and determine where they were going while they were at sea.

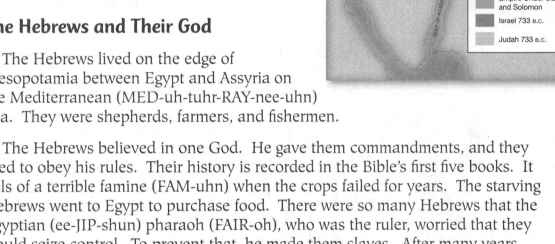

The Hebrews and Their God

The Hebrews lived on the edge of Mesopotamia between Egypt and Assyria on the Mediterranean (MED-uh-tuhr-RAY-nee-uhn) Sea. They were shepherds, farmers, and fishermen.

The Hebrews believed in one God. He gave them commandments, and they tried to obey his rules. Their history is recorded in the Bible's first five books. It tells of a terrible famine (FAM-uhn) when the crops failed for years. The starving Hebrews went to Egypt to purchase food. There were so many Hebrews that the Egyptian (ee-JIP-shun) pharaoh (FAIR-oh), who was the ruler, worried that they would seize control. To prevent that, he made them slaves. After many years, the slaves escaped from Egypt.

Tolerant Persians

The Persian (PURR-zhuhn) Empire was the largest in Mesopotamia from 539–330 B.C. It stretched from Egypt to India. The Persians were more tolerant than other conquerors. When they won a war, they let the defeated people maintain their worship practices and did not force them to change religions.

Cyrus (SY-ruhs) the Great was a Persian king who joined the kingdoms of Medes (MEED-uhs) and Persia. Cyrus conquered (KAHN-kuhrd) many civilizations, including Babylonia. He promised not to destroy the city of Babylon (BAB-uh-lawn) because he respected their religion and culture. Cyrus even repaired Babylon's temples.

35

The Babylonian ruler Nebuchadrezzar II (neb-yuh-kuh-DREZ-zuhr) had taken the Hebrews as slaves. In 539 B.C., Cyrus allowed the Hebrews to return to Jerusalem and helped to rebuild their temple in that city.

Fierce Assyrian Warriors

Assyria was a powerful empire in Mesopotamia. The Assyrians were fierce warriors who frequently battled to acquire more territory and enlarge the Assyrian Empire. They treated the people that they conquered poorly.

Like other empires and city-states, the Assyrian king was head of the army. Many of the men were soldiers. Other jobs included farmers and merchants. They were also poets, moneylenders, musicians, and scribes (men who could read and write).

✡	'aleph	[']	⌐	lamedh	[l]
ᔓ	beth	[b]	ᔓ	mem	[m]
ᄀ	gimel	[g]	ᄀ	nun	[n]
◁	daleth	[d]	‡	samekh	[s]
ᴲ	he	[h]	O	'ayin	[']
Y	waw	[w]	ᗑ	pe	[p]
⊥	zayin	[z]	ᒥ	tsade	[s]
⊟	heth	[h]	ᒍ	qoph	[q]
⊗	teth	[t]	◁	resh	[r]
⅄	yodh	[y]	W	shin	[sh]
ᴿ	caph	[k]	✕	taw	[t]

Talented Phoenicians

Another civilization in Mesopotamia belonged to the Phoenicians. The peak of their society came around 1000 B.C. These people were the first to make blown glass, and they created the first alphabet. They used snails to make rare purple dye and color expensive fabrics. Only royalty could afford to wear purple fabric.

The Phoenicians built wooden ships and sailed to Italy, Africa, and Spain. Wood was rare and desirable in this arid region, and the Phoenicians had cedar and pine forests. Thus, many people wanted to take their land. In 576 B.C., the Assyrians took over, and the Phoenician culture declined.

Comprehension Question

Give specific examples that show how these empires influence life today.

#50083 — *Leveled Texts: World Cultures*

Ancient Egypt

Nomads are people who move from place to place. About 5000 B.C., some nomads stopped moving around. They built homes. They lived along the Nile River. It is in North Africa. This river flooded each June. The flood lasted for four months. Then, the water went down. It left new soil on the bank of the river. It reached from the shore to six miles (about 10 km) inland.

This was rich soil. Grasses and reeds grew in it. Ducks and geese went there to eat. They built nests and laid eggs. Fish swam near the river's shore. The people found lots of food. The Nile River Valley was a good place to live.

The land near where the Nile River began was called Upper Egypt. The land near where the river met the Mediterranean (MED-uh-tuhr-RAY-nee-uhn) Sea had another name. It was called Lower Egypt.

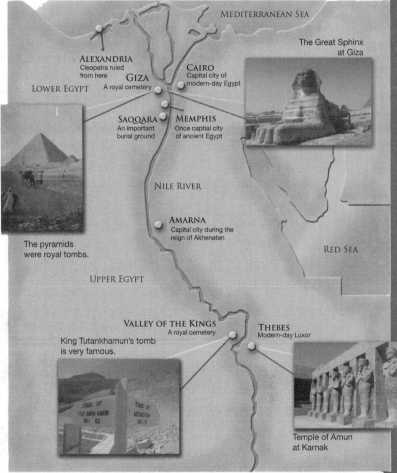

MEDITERRANEAN SEA

ALEXANDRIA
Cleopatra ruled from here

LOWER EGYPT

GIZA
A royal cemetery

CAIRO
Capital city of modern-day Egypt

The Great Sphinx at Giza

SAQQARA
An important burial ground

MEMPHIS
Once captial city of ancient Egypt

The pyramids were royal tombs.

NILE RIVER

AMARNA
Capital city during the reign of Akhenaten

RED SEA

UPPER EGYPT

VALLEY OF THE KINGS
A royal cemetery

King Tutankhamun's tomb is very famous.

THEBES
Modern-day Luxor

Temple of Amun at Karnak

Pharaohs

The pharaoh (FAIR-oh) was the ruler of Egypt. Every person had to obey him. What he said was the law. But, he did not have to follow any rules. He was seen as a god.

Brothers and sisters in the pharaoh's family married each other. This kept the family powerful. One by one, family members took the throne. Each one ruled until his death. A family holding power in this way is called a dynasty (DIE-nuhs-tee).

37

Egyptian Beliefs About Death

The Egyptians (ee-JIP-shunz) had many gods. Amun (AH-muhn) was the most important. He made all things. Thoth was a moon god. He ruled over learning. He also ruled over numbers. The sun god was Re (Ra). He was the "father of fathers." He was the "mother of mothers," too. The Egyptians said that each pharaoh was Re's child.

Egyptians believed in life after death. They thought that the dead would live again. A dead person's soul went to another world. It lived there with the gods and goddesses.

When a pharaoh died, his body was kept. It was made into a mummy. This took a long time. First, priests took out the organs. The heart stayed in the body. The body needed the heart to come back to life. The rest of the organs were put in special jars. They were called canopic (kuh-NO-pik) jars. The jars had lids. Each lid had a carved head. The head was a human, a jackal, a baboon, or a falcon. A jackal is a wild dog. A baboon is a monkey. A falcon is a hawk.

Then, the body was covered with natron. Natron is like salt. It dried the body so that it did not rot. Next, the priests wrapped the body in linen. Linen is a kind of cloth. They used 20 layers of cloth! The jewels of the dead person were put between these layers. Then, the body was laid in a fancy coffin. It was put in a secret room. The room held gold and treasures, too.

Comprehension Question

Name at least two ways the Nile River affected life in ancient Egypt.

38

Ancient Egypt

Around 5000 B.C., some nomads stopped moving around. They built homes along the Nile River in North Africa. Each year, starting in June, the Nile River flooded. The high water lasted about four months. It left new soil along the river's banks. This soil reached all the way from the river to about six miles (about 10 km) inland.

Grasses and reeds sprang up. Ducks and geese came to feed on them. They built nests and laid eggs. Fish swam near the river's shore. The settlers found lots of food in the Nile River Valley.

The lands near where the Nile River began were Upper Egypt. The lands near where the river drained into the Mediterranean (MED-uh-tuhr-RAY-nee-uhn) Sea were Lower Egypt.

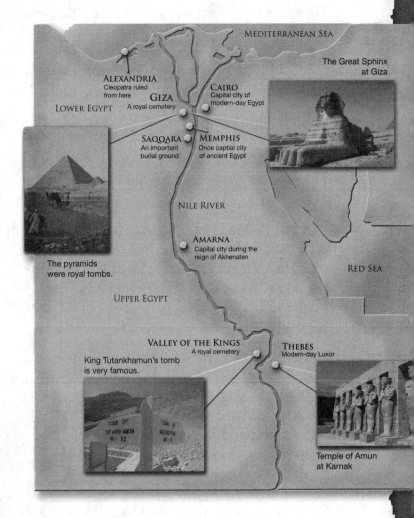

MEDITERRANEAN SEA

The Great Sphinx at Giza

ALEXANDRIA
Cleopatra ruled from here

LOWER EGYPT

GIZA
A royal cemetery

CAIRO
Capital city of modern-day Egypt

SAQQARA
An important burial ground

MEMPHIS
Once capital city of ancient Egypt

NILE RIVER

AMARNA
Capital city during the reign of Akhenaten

RED SEA

The pyramids were royal tombs.

UPPER EGYPT

VALLEY OF THE KINGS
A royal cemetery

King Tutankhamun's tomb is very famous.

THEBES
Modern-day Luxor

Temple of Amun at Karnak

Pharaohs

The pharaoh (FAIR-oh) was the ruler of Egypt. Every man, woman, and child in Egypt had to obey him. When he spoke, his words became law. But, there were no rules that he had to follow. He was seen as a god.

Brothers and sisters in the pharaoh's family married each other. This kept all the power in one family. One after another, family members would take the throne. A family holding power this way is called a dynasty (DIE-nuhs-tee).

39

Egyptian Beliefs About Death

The Egyptians (ee-JIP-shunz) had many gods. Amun (AH-muhn) was the most important. He created all things. There was a moon god, Thoth. He ruled over all learning. He also had control over numbers, weights, and measures. The sun god Re (also called Ra) was honored. He was called the "father of fathers" and the "mother of mothers." The Egyptians thought that each pharaoh was Re's child.

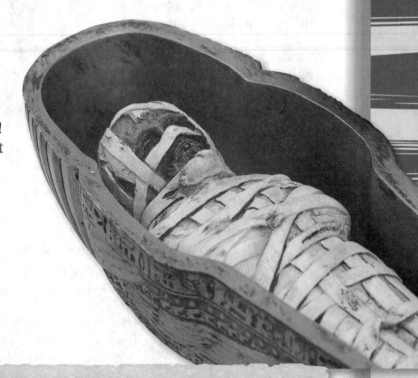

Egyptians believed in life after death. They thought that a dead person would live again. The dead person's spirit went to another world. There, it lived with the gods and goddesses. This is why the people turned their dead pharaohs into mummies.

It took a long time to make a mummy. First, priests took out the organs. The heart stayed in the body. It would be needed when the mummy returned to life. The other organs were put in canopic (kuh-NO-pik) jars. These special jars had lids. Each lid had a carved head. It was a human, a jackal, a baboon, or a falcon. A jackal is a wild dog. A baboon is a monkey. A falcon is a hawk.

The body was treated with natron. Natron is like baking soda. It dried the body. Then the body did not rot. Next, the priests wrapped the body in linen. Linen is cloth made from flax plants. They used 20 layers! The dead person's gems were put between these layers. Then, the body was laid in a fancy coffin. It was hidden in a burial room. The room held gold and other treasures, too.

Comprehension Question

Explain how the Nile River helped those living near it.

#50083—Leveled Texts: World Cultures

Ancient Egypt

Around 5000 B.C., nomads began to make homes along the Nile River in northern Africa. Each year, starting in June, the Nile River flooded. This flooding lasted about four months. It spread new soil all along the riverbanks. It stretched for about six miles (about 10 km) on both sides of the river.

Grasses and reeds sprang up. Ducks and geese came to feed on the grasses. They built nests and laid eggs. Fish swam in the shallow water near the edge of the Nile. The settlers found plenty of food in the Nile River Valley.

The lands near where the Nile River started were called Upper Egypt. The lands where the river emptied into the Mediterranean (MED-uh-tuhr-RAY-nee-uhn) Sea were called Lower Egypt.

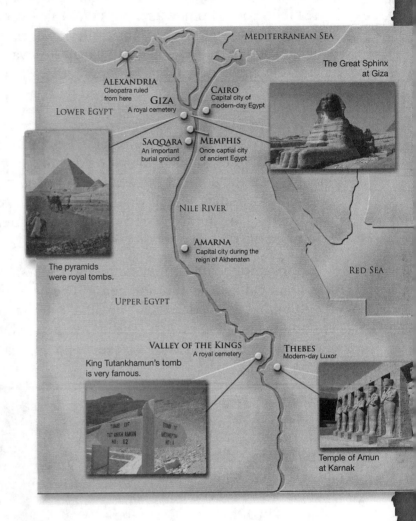

MEDITERRANEAN SEA

The Great Sphinx at Giza

ALEXANDRIA
Cleopatra ruled from here

CAIRO
Capital city of modern-day Egypt

GIZA
A royal cemetery

LOWER EGYPT

SAQQARA
An important burial ground

MEMPHIS
Once capital city of ancient Egypt

The pyramids were royal tombs.

NILE RIVER

AMARNA
Capital city during the reign of Akhenaten

RED SEA

UPPER EGYPT

VALLEY OF THE KINGS
A royal cemetery

King Tutankhamun's tomb is very famous.

THEBES
Modern-day Luxor

Temple of Amun at Karnak

Pharaohs

The pharaoh (FAIR-oh) was the most important person in Egypt. Every man, woman, and child in Egypt knew of the pharaoh's power. When the pharaoh said something, his words became law. But, there were no laws that the pharaoh had to obey. He was seen as a god.

It was common for brothers and sisters in the pharaoh's family to marry each other. This kept power in the ruler's family. One after another, family members would take the throne. A family holding power in this way is called a dynasty (DIE-nuhs-tee).

41

Egyptian Beliefs About Death

The Egyptians (ee-JIP-shunz) had many gods. Amun (AH-muhn) was the name of the Egyptians' most important god. The moon god, Thoth, was believed to rule over all learning. Egyptians respected him for his control over numbers, weights, and measures. Re (also called Ra) was the sun god. He was worshipped as the "father of fathers" and the "mother of mothers." The Egyptians believed that each pharaoh was Re's child.

Egyptians wanted to live forever. They believed that a well-kept corpse would awaken one day to live again. They thought that the spirit of the dead person would travel to another world. There, it would live with the gods and goddesses. Due to these beliefs, they turned their dead rulers into mummies.

It took a long time to make a mummy. First, embalmers removed all the vital organs except for the heart. The heart would be needed when the mummy returned to life. The other internal organs were placed in canopic (kuh-NO-pik) jars. These special jars had fancy lids. Each lid had a carved head of a human, a jackal (wild dog), a baboon (monkey), or a falcon (hawk).

The body was then covered with natron. Natron is similar to baking soda. Then, the priests wrapped the body in linen. Linen is fabric made from flax plant fibers. The body was wrapped in 20 layers! Often the dead person's jewels were placed between the layers. The body was laid in a decorated casket and hidden in a burial chamber that also held gold and treasures.

Comprehension Question

Why was living near the Nile River ideal for the people of ancient Egypt?

42

Ancient Egypt

Around 5000 B.C., some nomads decided to stop wandering and made their homes along the Nile River in northern Africa. Every year, starting in June, the Nile River flooded. This flooding lasted about four months. When the water receded, it deposited new soil along the riverbanks for about six miles (about 10 km) inland.

Grasses and reeds sprang up. The ducks and geese that came to feed on the grasses built nests and laid eggs. Fish swam in the shallow water near the Nile's shores. The settlers found plenty of food in the Nile River Valley.

The lands near the head, or beginning, of the Nile River were called Upper Egypt. Lower Egypt referred to the lands where the river emptied into the Mediterranean (MED-uh-tuhr-RAY-nee-uhn) Sea.

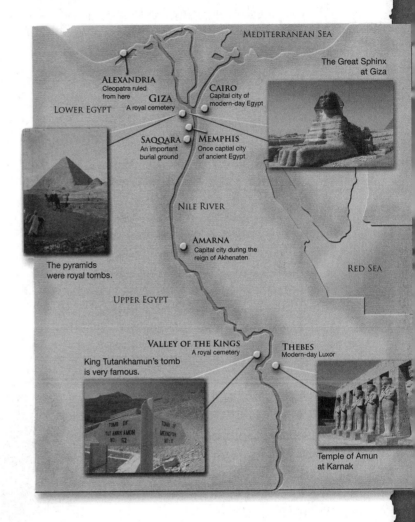

MEDITERRANEAN SEA

The Great Sphinx at Giza

ALEXANDRIA
Cleopatra ruled from here

LOWER EGYPT

GIZA
A royal cemetery

CAIRO
Capital city of modern-day Egypt

SAQQARA
An important burial ground

MEMPHIS
Once captial city of ancient Egypt

NILE RIVER

The pyramids were royal tombs.

AMARNA
Capital city during the reign of Akhenaten

RED SEA

UPPER EGYPT

VALLEY OF THE KINGS
A royal cemetery

King Tutankhamun's tomb is very famous.

THEBES
Modern-day Luxor

Temple of Amun at Karnak

Pharaohs

The pharaoh (FAIR-oh) was the most important person in Egypt. Every man, woman, and child in Egypt respected his power. When the pharaoh said something, his words became law. Yet no laws bound the pharaoh. He did not have to obey rules, for he was like a god.

The brothers and sisters in the pharaoh's family often married each other. This kept power in the ruler's family because one after another, family members would take the throne. A family holding power in this way is called a dynasty (DIE-nuhs-tee).

43

Egyptian Beliefs About Death

The Egyptians (ee-JIP-shunz) had many gods. Amun (AH-muhn) was the Egyptians' most important god because he had created everything. The moon god, Thoth, ruled over all learning and controlled numbers, weights, and measures. The sun god Re (also called Ra) was worshipped as the "father of fathers" and the "mother of mothers." The Egyptians believed that every pharaoh was Re's child.

Egyptians wanted to live forever, and they believed that a corpse would awaken one day to live again. They thought that the dead person's spirit would travel to another world to live with the gods and goddesses. Based on these beliefs, they turned their pharaohs' dead bodies into mummies.

It took a long time to make a mummy. First, embalmers removed all the vital organs. Only the heart remained in the body because it would be needed for the mummy to return to life. All other internal organs were placed in canopic (kuh-NO-pik) jars. These special jars had lids carved with the head of a human, a jackal (wild dog), a baboon (monkey), or a falcon (hawk).

Then the body was covered with natron, a substance similar to baking soda. It dried the body and prevented decay. Next, priests wrapped the body in 20 layers of linen, placing the dead person's jewels between the layers. Linen is fabric made from flax plant fibers. Finally, the body was laid in a decorated casket and hidden in a burial chamber that also held all the other treasures the deceased would need in his next life.

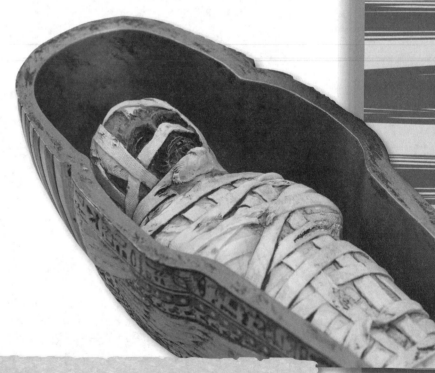

Comprehension Question

List at least three reasons the nomads decided to settle near the Nile River.

44

Rulers of Egypt

The Egyptians (ee-JIP-shunz) lived along the Nile River. It is the longest river on Earth. Egypt was a long, narrow nation. It was hard to keep it safe. Only the best pharaohs (FAIR-ohz) could keep their enemies out. There were times when other groups took some of Egypt's land.

About 1730 B.C., an army came from Asia. It marched into northern Egypt. The Hyksos (HIK-saws) took over the Nile Delta. They moved into the Nile River Valley. The Hyksos held large parts of Egypt. They held it for more than 100 years.

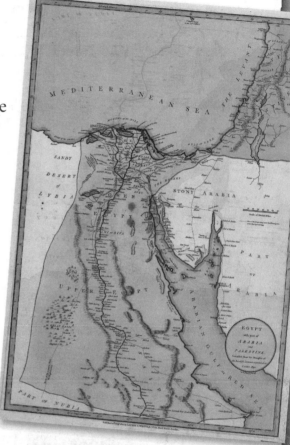

Ahmose I (AH-mohs the first) drove out the Hyksos. They went back to Asia. But, they had an effect on the Egyptians. Their ideas and customs stayed there. When they left, there was peace. Ahmose was a strong ruler.

Hatshepsut, A Female Pharaoh

About 1518 B.C., Pharaoh Thutmose I (THUHT-mohs the first) took the throne. He and his queen had four children. Three died. Just one grew up. Her name was Hatshepsut. When she was a teenager, her father died. But she could not take his place. The ruler had to be a man.

Thutmose had a son with another wife. So, Thutmose II became the new ruler. Hatshepsut acted as his regent (REE-juhnt) for ten years. A regent is a person who rules while the pharaoh is young, absent, or ill. Thutmose II died young. Then, Thutmose III became pharaoh. He was a small child. He could not keep his regent from taking over. After about seven years, Hatshepsut grew tired of ruling for others. She made herself pharaoh. She ruled for 22 years. When she died, Thutmose III took the throne. He was a strong ruler.

Other Rulers

Akhenaten (aw-kuh-NAW-tuhn) ruled from about 1379 to 1362 B.C. Next came Tutankhamun (toot-ank-AH-muhn). He took over when he was about nine years old. He died as a teenager. But his name is well known. A lot of treasures were found in his tomb.

Ramses II (RAM-seez the second) ruled for a long time. He fought for years to keep the Hittites (HIT-tites) out. During times of peace, he built big temples. They were in the cities of Egypt.

Egypt Is Taken Over

The Persians (PURR-zhuhnz) had control of Egypt by 525 B.C. They ruled for nearly 200 years. Then, in 332 B.C., Alexander the Great and his Greek army came. They took over. They ruled most of the known world. But the Egyptians were glad! They hated the Persians.

By this time, the Roman Empire was growing. It spread through Europe, Asia, and Africa. The Romans came to Egypt. They took over. In 30 B.C., Egypt was made part of the Roman Empire. It was a province. A province is like a state. It is a part of a bigger nation.

The Egyptian civilization (siv-uh-luh-ZAY-shuhn) had lasted for 3,000 years. But now it was over.

Comprehension Question

What made Hatshepsut a special ruler in Egypt?

Rulers of Egypt

It was hard to keep enemies out of Egypt. The people lived along the Nile. It is the longest river on Earth. It was tough to protect such a long, narrow nation. Only the strongest and wisest of rulers could keep the borders safe. So at times, people from other places took over some of Egypt's land.

About 1730 B.C., an army from Asia came into northern Egypt. The Hyksos (HIK-saws) conquered (KAHN-kuhrd) the Nile Delta at the Mediterranean (MED-uh-tuhr-RAY-nee-uhn) Sea. Then, they moved into the Nile River Valley. The Hyksos held large parts of Egypt. This lasted for more than 100 years.

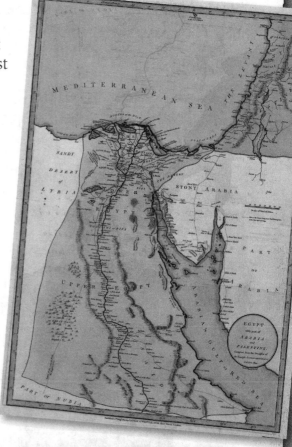

Ahmose I (AH-mohs the first) drove out the Hyksos. Yet, influences from them remained part of Egyptian (ee-JIP-shun) life. After the Hyksos left Egypt, there was a time of peace. Ahmose was a strong ruler.

Hatshepsut, A Female Pharaoh

About 1518 B.C., Thutmose I (THUHT-mohs the first) took the throne. He and his queen had two sons and two daughters. But just one child lived to adulthood. Her name was Hatshepsut. When she was a teenager, her father, the pharaoh (FAIR-oh), died.

Thutmose had a son with another wife. So, Thutmose II became the new pharaoh. For ten years, Hatshepsut acted as his regent (REE-juhnt). A regent is a person who rules while the pharaoh is too young, absent, or ill. Thutmose II died young. In about 1504 B.C., Thutmose III became pharaoh. But he was young. He could not keep his regent from taking over. After about seven years, Hatshepsut made herself pharaoh. She ruled for 22 years. When she died, Thutmose III took the throne. He was a strong pharaoh.

#50083 — Leveled Texts: World Cultures

Other Rulers

Akhenaten (aw-kuh-NAW-tuhn) ruled from about 1379 to 1362 B.C. Next came Tutankhamun (toot-ank-AH-muhn). He took the throne when he was about nine years old. He died as a teen. But he is well known. People remember him because of the treasures found in his tomb.

Ramses II (RAM-seez the second) had a long reign. He spent years fighting to keep the Hittites (HIT-tites) out of Egypt. During times of peace, he built big temples in Egypt's cities.

Egypt Is Taken Over

By 525 B.C., the Persians (PURR-zhuhnz) seized control of Egypt. They ruled for nearly 200 years. In 332 B.C., Alexander the Great and his Greek army took over Egypt. In fact, they took over most of the known world. The Egyptians were glad! They hated the Persians.

By this time, the Roman Empire was growing. It spread through Europe, Asia, and Africa. The Romans attacked Egypt. In 30 B.C., it became a Roman Empire province. A province is a part of a larger nation or empire. The Egyptian civilization (siv-uh-luh-ZAY-shuhn) lasted 3,000 years. Now, it was over.

Comprehension Question

How did Hatshepsut get the chance to rule?

#50083— *Leveled Texts: World Cultures*

Rulers of Egypt

It was hard to protect Egypt from enemies because its citizens lived along the Nile, the longest river on Earth. The army struggled to protect a country so long and narrow. Only the strongest and wisest of pharaohs (FAIR-ohz) could secure the country's borders. So at times, people from other nations took over some of Egypt's land.

About 1730 B.C., invaders (in-VADE-uhrz) from Asia took over northern Egypt. The Hyksos (HIK-saws) conquered (KAHN-kuhrd) the Nile Delta at the Mediterranean (MED-uh-tuhr-RAY-nee-uhn) Sea. Then, they moved into the Nile River Valley. The Hyksos held large parts of Egypt for more than 100 years.

Ahmose I (AH-mohs) was finally able to drive out the Hyksos. However, many influences from these invaders remained part of Egyptian (ee-JIP-shun) life. After the Hyksos left Egypt, there was a time of peace. Ahmose was a strong leader.

Hatshepsut, A Female Pharaoh

In about 1518 B.C., Pharaoh Thutmose I (THUHT-mohs) took the throne. He and his queen had four children. They had two sons and two daughters, but just one of them lived to adulthood. Her name was Hatshepsut. When she was a teen, her father (the pharaoh) died.

Thutmose I had a son with a different wife. So, Thutmose II became pharaoh. Hatshepsut served as his regent (REE-juhnt) for ten years. A regent is a person who rules while the heir to the throne is too young, absent, or ill. Thutmose II died young and left Egypt's throne without a pharaoh.

In about 1504 B.C., Thutmose III became pharaoh. But, he was too young to keep Hatshepsut from making the decisions about how Egypt would be ruled. After about seven years, she declared herself pharaoh. She took the throne and ruled Egypt for about 22 years. When she died, Thutmose III became a strong, well-respected pharaoh.

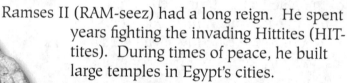

Other Rulers

Akhenaten (aw-kuh-NAW-tuhn) was Egypt's pharaoh from about 1379 to 1362 B.C. Next came Tutankhamun (toot-ank-AH-muhn), who took the throne when he was about nine years old. He died as a teenager but is well known because of the treasures found in his tomb.

Ramses II (RAM-seez) had a long reign. He spent years fighting the invading Hittites (HIT-tites). During times of peace, he built large temples in Egypt's cities.

Egypt Is Taken Over

By 525 B.C., the powerful Persians (PURR-zhuhnz) moved into Egypt. They ruled Egypt for nearly 200 years. In 332 B.C., Alexander the Great and his Greek army conquered Egypt and most of the known world. The Egyptians actually welcomed him because they hated the Persians.

By this time, the Roman Empire was expanding through Europe, Asia, and Africa. Egypt was attacked, and in 30 B.C., it became a province of the mighty Roman Empire. A province is a part of a larger nation or empire. The Egyptian civilization (siv-uh-luh-ZAY-shuhn) had lasted 3,000 years.

Comprehension Question

What made it possible for Hatshepsut to rule as a pharaoh?

Rulers of Egypt

Protecting Egypt from invading armies was difficult because its citizens lived along the Nile, the longest river on Earth. The Egyptian (ee-JIP-shun) army struggled to secure the borders of a country so long and narrow, and only the strongest and wisest pharaohs (FAIR-ohz) could repel invasions. Thus, at times, people from other nations took over some of Egypt's land.

About 1730 B.C., Asian invaders (in-VADE-uhrz) took over northern Egypt and conquered (KAHN-kuhrd) the Nile Delta at the Mediterranean (MED-uh-tuhr-RAY-nee-uhn) Sea. Then, the Hyksos (HIK-saws) moved into the Nile River Valley and held large parts of Egypt for more than 100 years.

Ahmose I (AH-mohs) was able to drive out the Hyksos, but these invaders left behind many influences that continued to remain part of Egyptian life. After the Hyksos left Egypt, there was a time of peace because Ahmose I was a strong leader.

Hatshepsut, A Female Pharaoh

In about 1518 B.C., Pharaoh Thutmose I (THUHT-mohs) took the throne. He and his queen had two sons and two daughters, but just one of them lived to adulthood. Her name was Hatshepsut, and when she was a teen, her father (the pharaoh) died.

Thutmose I had a son with a different wife, and so, Thutmose II became pharaoh. Hatshepsut served as his regent (REE-juhnt) for ten years. A regent is a person who rules while the heir to the throne is too young, absent, or ill. Thutmose II died young and left Egypt's throne without a pharaoh.

51

In about 1504 B.C., Thutmose III became pharaoh when he was too young to keep Hatshepsut from controlling Egypt. After about seven years of being his regent, she declared herself pharaoh and ruled Egypt for about 22 years. After her death, Thutmose III became a strong, well-respected pharaoh.

Other Rulers

Akhenaten (aw-kuh-NAW-tuhn) was Egypt's pharaoh from about 1379 to 1362 B.C. Next came Tutankhamun (toot-ank-AH-muhn), who took the throne when he was about nine years old. He died as a teenager, but he is well known because of the treasures found in his intact tomb.

Ramses II (RAM-seez) had a long reign and spent years fighting the invading Hittites (HIT-tites). During times of peace, he built elaborate temples throughout Egypt's cities.

Egypt Is Taken Over

By 525 B.C., the powerful Persians (PURR-zhuhnz) moved into Egypt and ruled the nation for nearly 200 years. In 332 B.C., Alexander the Great and his Greek army conquered Egypt and most of the known world. The Egyptians actually welcomed him because they hated the Persians.

By this time, the Roman Empire was expanding through Europe, Asia, and Africa. Egypt was attacked, and in 30 B.C., it became a province of the mighty Roman Empire. A province is a part of a larger nation or empire. The Egyptian civilization (siv-uh-luh-ZAY-shuhn) that had lasted for 3,000 years was over.

Comprehension Question

Describe the circumstances that allowed Hatshepsut to rule Egypt.

Ancient Greece

The mainland of Greece is located on the southern tip of Europe. It is hot and dry. It has mountains. Three bodies of water surround it. They are the Aegean (ih-JEE-uhn), Adriatic (ay-dree-AT-ik), and Mediterranean (MED-uh-tuhr-RAY-nee-uhn) Seas. Greece also owns the small islands around it.

Long ago, Greece was bigger. Greece had colonies from the eighth to the fifth centuries B.C. They were in southern Italy. Some of them were on the shores of the Black Sea. There were others in the western part of the Mediterranean, too. The people in these colonies built Greek homes. They made pots in the Greek style. So, the Greek way of life had an effect in these places.

Greek Religion

The Greeks had many gods. Poseidon (puh-SY-duhn) was god of the seas and rivers. Apollo (uh-PAWL-lo) ruled the sun and light. He knew the future. Aphrodite (ahf-ruh-DIE-tee) was goddess of love and beauty. The goddess of war and wisdom was Athena (uh-THEE-nuh).

The gods were in charge of people's lives. The Greeks prayed to the gods often. This helped them make choices about how to fight a war. It helped them choose whom to marry. Even small choices were made in this way.

Art and Theater

The Greeks were artists. They made statues. They built temples for the gods. These temples were painted yellow, red, and blue. Their walls had huge paintings. Today, parts of these buildings remain. But the paint is gone.

The Greeks wrote plays. Early plays were about the gods. The city-state of Athens held the first public plays. They were presented in open-air theaters. These were shaped like half circles. They had seats built right into the hillside.

53

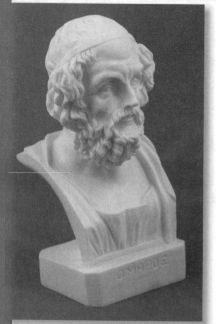

Science and Medicine

The Greeks liked science. They found out things about math, plants, animals, and the stars. They studied nature. They were the first people in Europe to base their ideas on what they saw in nature.

Medicine was an important science. At first, the Greeks thought that illness was a punishment from the gods. So, they built holy places to honor the god of medicine. Sick people spent the night at these holy places. They prayed for a cure. Later, the Greeks came up with treatments for the sick. Hippocrates (hip-PAWK-ruh-teez) thought of many of the treatments. That's why he is called the Father of Modern Medicine.

Philosophers

Socrates (SAWK-ruh-teez) was the first Greek philosopher. He tried to figure out the meaning of life. He asked questions about a topic. This way he got others to share their thoughts. It is called the Socratic (suh-KRAT-ik) Method.

Plato was his pupil. He wrote down Socrates' ideas. That is how we know about them. Plato began a school after Socrates died. Aristotle (AIR-uh-stawt-uhl) learned from Plato for 20 years. When Plato died, Aristotle had his own school. He taught science.

Comprehension Question

Pick one part of Greek life and describe how it ties to today.

#50083—Leveled Texts: World Cultures

Ancient Greece

The country of Greece lies on Europe's southern tip. It borders the Aegean (ih-JEE-uhn), Adriatic (ay-dree-AT-ik), and Mediterranean (MED-uh-tuhr-RAY-nee-uhn) Seas. Greece has a mainland. Small islands surround it. This hot, dry country has mountains.

From the eighth to the fifth centuries B.C., Greece was bigger than today. The Greeks had colonies in southern Italy. To the east, they had colonies on the Black Sea's shore. They were in the western part of the Mediterranean, too. Even in the colonies far from Greece, the people built cities and made pottery in the Greek style. So, the Greek way of life had an effect on many places.

Greek Religion

The Greeks believed in many gods. Poseidon (puh-SY-duhn) was the god of the seas and rivers. Apollo (uh-PAWL-lo) ruled the sun and light. He could tell the future. Aphrodite (ahf-ruh-DIE-tee) was the goddess of love and beauty. Athena (uh-THEE-nuh) was the goddess of war and wisdom.

The Greeks thought that the gods ruled every part of people's lives. Choices about war and marriage were made after checking with the gods. Even small choices in life were made this way.

Art and Theater

The Greeks made statues. They built beautiful temples for the gods. These temples were painted yellow, red, and blue. The walls had huge paintings, or murals. Parts of these buildings remain, but now the paint is gone.

The Greeks wrote plays. Early Greek plays were about religion. Later plays had to do with politics. In 534 B.C., Athens held the first public plays. They were done in open-air theaters shaped like semicircles. Seats were built right into the hillside. Some ancient Greek plays are still performed.

#50083 — Leveled Texts: World Cultures

Science and Medicine

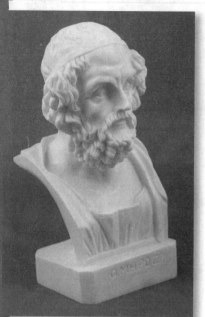

The Greeks were interested in science. They learned new things about living beings, math, and the stars. They were the first people in Europe to base what they knew on what they saw in nature.

Medicine was an important Greek science. At first, the Greeks thought that illness was a punishment from the gods. They built holy places to honor the god of medicine. People would spend the night at a holy place. They would pray for a cure. Later, the Greeks came up with treatments for the sick. Hippocrates (hip-PAWK-ruh-teez) thought of many of the treatments. He is called the Father of Modern Medicine.

Philosophers

Socrates (SAWK-ruh-teez) was the first Greek philosopher. He tried to figure out the meaning of life. He asked many questions about a subject. In this way, he got others to share their knowledge. This is called the Socratic (suh-KRAT-ik) Method.

Plato was Socrates' pupil. He wrote down Socrates' ideas. That is how we know about them. After Socrates died, Plato started a school. Aristotle (AIR-uh-stawt-uhl) studied under Plato for 20 years. When Plato died, Aristotle started his own school.

Comprehension Question

Pick at least two parts of Greek life. Describe how each influences life today.

#50083 — Leveled Texts: World Cultures

Ancient Greece

Greece is located on the southern tip of Europe. It borders the Aegean (ih-JEE-uhn), Adriatic (ay-dree-AT-ik), and Mediterranean (MED-uh-tuhr-RAY-nee-uhn) Seas. Greece has a large mainland surrounded by many smaller islands. It is a hot, dry country with mountain ranges.

From the eighth to the fifth centuries B.C., Greece stretched beyond its current borders. The Greeks built colonies in southern Italy and around the western part of the Mediterranean. They also moved east to the coast of the Black Sea. Even in the colonies farthest away from Greece, the colonists built cities and made pottery in the Greek style. Thus, Greek culture had a great influence on many of these areas.

Greek Religion

Greek life centered on religion. Greeks worshipped many gods and thought that they controlled every part of people's lives. Decisions about war and marriage were made after checking with the gods. Even minor decisions were made the same way.

Poseidon (puh-SY-duhn) was the god of the seas and rivers. Apollo (uh-PAWL-lo) controlled the sun and light and could predict the future. Aphrodite (ahf-ruh-DIE-tee) was the goddess of love and beauty. Athena (uh-THEE-nuh) was the goddess of war and wisdom.

Art and Theater

The Greeks created statues and beautiful temples dedicated to the gods. The temples were painted yellow, red, and blue. Huge wall paintings, called murals, decorated these buildings. The ruins of these buildings remain, but the paint wore away long ago.

Early Greek plays had religious themes. Later plays began to deal with politics. In 534 B.C., the first public plays were held in Athens. They were performed in open-air theaters shaped like semicircles. Seats were built into the hillsides. Some ancient Greek plays are still performed.

57

Science and Medicine

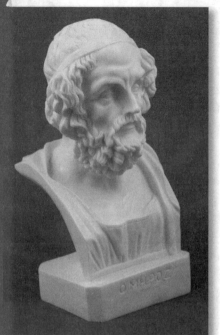

The Greeks were interested in science. They made advances in biology, mathematics, astronomy, and geography. They were the first people in Europe to base what they knew on what they observed in the world.

An important area of Greek science was medicine. In the beginning, the Greeks believed that illness was a punishment from the gods. Sanctuaries (SANK-chuh-wear-eez), which are holy places to honor the god of medicine, were built all over Greece. People would spend the night at a sanctuary and pray for a cure. Later, the Greeks designed treatments for diseases. Hippocrates (hip-PAWK-ruh-teez) developed many of these treatments based on his research. He is called the Father of Modern Medicine.

Philosophers

Socrates (SAWK-ruh-teez) was the first Greek philosopher. A philosopher tries to figure out the meaning of life. He asked many questions about a subject. In this way he prompted others to share their knowledge. This is called the Socratic (suh-KRAT-ik) Method. Plato was Socrates' pupil. He recorded Socrates' ideas, which is how we know about them. After Socrates died, Plato started a school. Aristotle (AIR-uh-stawt-uhl) was a philosopher and a scientist who studied under Plato for 20 years. When Plato died, Aristotle started his own school.

Comprehension Question

How do ancient Greek successes affect life today?

#50083—Leveled Texts: World Cultures   © Shell Education

Ancient Greece

Located on the southern tip of Europe, the nation of Greece is bordered by the Aegean (ih-JEE-uhn), Adriatic (ay-dree-AT-ik), and Mediterranean (MED-uh-tuhr-RAY-nee-uhn) Seas. Islands surround the Greece mainland. This hot, dry nation has mountain ranges.

During the eighth to the fifth centuries B.C., Greece spread beyond its current borders. Some Greeks settled in southern Italy, while others began colonies near the western part of the Mediterranean. To the east, they built colonies on the Black Sea's coast. Although these colonies were far from Greece, the colonists practiced Greek traditions. As a result, Greek culture had a lasting influence on many of these regions.

Greek Religion

The Greeks worshipped many gods and thought that they controlled people's lives. Decisions about war and marriage were made only after checking with the gods, and even minor decisions were made in this way.

Poseidon (puh-SY-duhn) was the god of the seas and rivers. Apollo (uh-PAWL-lo) not only controlled the sun and light, he predicted the future. Aphrodite (ahf-ruh-DIE-tee) was the goddess of love and beauty. Athena (uh-THEE-nuh) was the goddess of war and wisdom. The city of Athens was named for her and the beautiful Parthenon was built in her honor.

Art and Theater

The Greeks created beautiful statues and temples dedicated to the gods. Colorful murals decorated the temple walls. Although the paint has worn away, the ruins of these magnificent buildings remain.

Early Greek plays had religious themes, but later plays had political themes. In 534 B.C., the first public plays were performed in Athens in open-air theaters shaped like semicircles. The audience sat in seats built into the hillside. Some ancient Greek plays are still performed today.

59

Science and Medicine

The Greeks were the first Europeans to base their knowledge on what they observed in the natural world. They made major advances in biology, mathematics, astronomy, and geography.

Initially the Greeks believed that illness was always a punishment from the gods. Holy places called sanctuaries (SANK-chuh-wear-eez) were built to honor the god of medicine. Sick people spent the night inside a sanctuary praying for a cure. Later, the Greeks designed treatments for diseases based on research done by Hippocrates (hip-PAWK-ruh-teez), who is called the Father of Modern Medicine.

Philosophers

Socrates (SAWK-ruh-teez) was the first philosopher. Philosophers want to understand existence and its meaning. Socrates created the Socratic (suh-KRAT-ik) Method in which he asked multiple questions about a subject as a way to prompt others to share their knowledge. Plato was Socrates' pupil. He recorded Socrates' ideas, which is how we know about them. After Socrates died, Plato started a school. Plato's student, Aristotle (AIR-uh-stawt-uhl), was a scientist and philosopher. When Plato died, Aristotle started his own school.

Comprehension Question

Describe the influence ancient Greeks have on life today.

Greek City-States

In the eighth century B.C., army leaders ruled small parts of Greece. Rich families ruled other parts. These places were called city-states or poleis (PAW-lays). The men in each city-state had rights. But no one else did. Women and children had no rights. Men from other places and slaves had no rights.

Some city-states were democracies. This meant that the men had the right to vote. They chose their leaders. They had a say in how things were done. Such governments are still rare today.

The Minoans and Mycenaeans

The Minoans (muh-NO-uhnz) lived on Crete (KREET). It is an island. They had good land. Crops grew well. So, the Minoans had enough to eat. And, they had food left over for trade. They traded with other Greeks. They traded with people in Egypt. They traded with other groups, too.

The Mycenaeans (my-suh-NEE-uhnz) lived on the mainland. They were there at the height of the Minoan society. The Mycenaeans made things by hand. Then they sold them. They had a strong army. Even so, invaders (in-VADE-uhrz) attacked them. By 1000 B.C., their society was gone.

Athens and Sparta

There were many city-states. We know the most about Athens and Sparta. People left records. They wrote the history of these city-states. They told about their daily lives.

The cities of Athens and Sparta were not the same. The people of Athens valued freedom. They loved beauty. They liked learning new things. Writers, artists, and builders lived there.

The army led Sparta. It was known for its brave soldiers. All males had to serve in the army. This city-state owned each boy from birth. In Sparta, working hard, never giving up, and doing your duty were important. It was an honor to die for Sparta.

Greek Wars

The Greeks fought many wars. Sometimes, they had battles with people who wanted to take their land. Other times they fought with each other. They fought the Persians (PURR-zhuhnz) for almost 50 years. The Persians hoped to take over Greece. The fighting went on and on. At last, Athens' navy stopped the Persians for good. But then, Athens and Sparta turned on each other! They fought for 27 years. Sparta won. But, both city-states ended up weaker.

The Greek leader Alexander the Great led a strong army in 334 B.C. He wanted to build the biggest empire in the world. He did just that. First, he took over Persia. Egypt was next. Then, he held parts of the Indus Valley.

Alexander the Great wanted to bring Greek culture to new places. Scientists, artists, and poets went along with his troops. At one time, Alexander had a huge empire. It reached from Greece to northern India.

Comprehension Question

Why do we know a lot about
Athens and Sparta?

Greek City-States

In the eighth century B.C., military leaders led small parts of Greece. Rich families ruled others. These parts were called city-states or poleis (PAW-lays). They had two groups of people. The men had rights. They even made decisions. The rest of the people had no rights. This included women, children, slaves, and people from other places.

Some city-states had a special kind of government. It was called democracy. This meant that the men voted for their leaders. Such governments were not common. But, they were used in ancient Greece.

The Minoans and Mycenaeans

The Minoans (muh-NO-uhnz) had the first great culture in Greece. They lived on the island of Crete (KREET). Their land grew good crops. They traded with other Greeks. They traded with Egypt and other nations, too.

The Mycenaean (my-suh-NEE-uhn) people came around 1600 B.C. They lived on the mainland. They were there at the height of the Minoan society. The Mycenaeans worked as craftsmen and traders. They made things by hand and sold them. They had a strong army. Even so, about 1250 B.C. invaders (in-VADE-uhrz) attacked them. By 1000 B.C., their society was gone.

Athens and Sparta

We know the most about the city-states of Athens and Sparta. The men who lived there left records. They wrote the history of these city-states. They also wrote about daily life.

The cultures of Athens and Sparta were not the same. Athens reached its height in the mid-fifth century B.C. The people of Athens valued beauty and freedom. They liked the search for knowledge. Writers, artists, and builders made their homes there.

The army led Sparta. It was well known for its brave troops. All males had to serve. Each boy belonged to the city-state at birth. In Sparta, working hard, never giving up, and doing your duty were the most important traits. To a Spartan, it was an honor to die for Sparta.

Greek Wars

The Greeks fought many wars. Sometimes they fought invaders. At other times, they fought with each other. For almost 50 years, they joined forces to battle the Persians (PURR-zhuhnz). The Persians kept trying to take over Greece. The fighting went on and on. At last, Athens' navy stopped them. But then, Athens and Sparta turned on each other! They fought from 431–404 B.C. The Spartans won. But both city-states ended up weaker.

In 334 B.C., the Greek leader Alexander the Great led a strong army. He set out to build the world's largest empire. He did just that. First he took over Persia. Egypt was next. Then, he held parts of the Indus Valley. He wanted to bring Greek culture to new places. He had scientists, artists, and poets go along with his troops. At one time, Alexander had a huge empire. It reached from Greece to northern India.

Comprehension Question

Describe life in either Athens or Sparta.

#50083—*Leveled Texts: World Cultures*

Greek City-States

In the eighth century B.C., military leaders and wealthy families ruled small parts of Greece. These poleis (PAW-lays), or city-states, had two kinds of people. Adult males were citizens, and they made all the decisions. The rest were women, children, foreigners, and slaves. As noncitizens, they had no rights.

Some poleis, such as Athens, had democracies, which meant that men voted for their leaders. These governments were unique to ancient Greece.

The Minoans and Mycenaeans

The Minoans (muh-NO-uhnz) had the first great culture in Greece. They lived on the island of Crete (KREET). Their land grew good crops. They traded with other parts of Greece and other nations, including Egypt.

The Mycenaean (my-suh-NEE-uhn) people arrived around 1600 B.C. They lived on the Greek mainland during the height of the Minoan civilization (siv-uh-luh-ZAY-shuhn). The Mycenaeans were craftsmen and traders. Even though they had a strong army, invaders (in-VADE-uhrz) attacked them around 1250 B.C. By 1000 B.C., their civilization had vanished.

Athens and Sparta

Athens and Sparta are the two ancient Greek city-states about which we know the most. The men who lived there left records about their culture and traditions.

The cultures of Athens and Sparta were quite different. Athens reached its height in the mid-fifth century B.C. The people of Athens valued beauty and freedom. They enjoyed the quest for knowledge.

Α	Β	Γ	Δ	Ε	Ζ
Alpha	Beta	Gamma	Delta	Epsilon	Zeta
Η	Θ	Ι	Κ	Λ	Μ
Eta	Theta	Iota	Kappa	Lambda	Mu
Ν	Ξ	Ο	Π	Ρ	Σ
Ni	Xi	Omicron	Pi	Rho	Sigma
Τ	Υ	Φ	Χ	Ψ	Ω
Tau	Upsilon	Phi	Chi	Psi	Omega

The army led Sparta. It was well known for its brave troops. All males had to serve in the military. Each boy belonged to the city-state at birth. In Sparta, working hard, never giving up, and doing your duty were the most valued traits. To a Spartan, it was an honor to die for Sparta.

Greek Wars

The Greeks fought many wars. For nearly 50 years they battled the Persians (PURR-zhuhnz). The Persians kept attacking because they wanted to take over Greece. At last, Athens' navy stopped them once and for all. But then, Athens and Sparta turned on each other and fought the Peloponnesian (PEL-uh-puh-NEE-shuhn) War from 431–404 B.C. The Spartans won. Both city-states were weakened.

In 334 B.C., the Greek leader Alexander the Great had a strong army. He wanted to create the world's largest empire—and he did. First he took over Persia. Egypt was next. Then, he seized parts of the Indus Valley. He wanted to bring Greek culture to these places. So, scientists, artists, and poets traveled with his troops. At one time, Alexander held a huge empire. It stretched from Greece to northern India.

Comprehension Question

Compare and contrast life in Athens and Sparta.

#50083—*Leveled Texts: World Cultures*

Greek City-States

Around the eighth century B.C., military leaders and rich families ruled small parts of Greece. These poleis (PAW-lays), or city-states, had citizens and noncitizens. The citizens were adult males. They made all the major decisions. The others had no rights. These included women, children, foreigners, and slaves.

Over time, Athens and some other poleis developed democratic governments. Male citizens voted for their leaders. Such democracies were unique to ancient Greek culture.

The Minoans and Mycenaeans

The Minoan (muh-NO-uhn) civilization (siv-uh-luh-ZAY-shuhn) was the first great culture of ancient Greece. The Minoans lived on the island of Crete (KREET). They had fertile land that produced great crops. They also traded with other parts of Greece and other nations, including Egypt.

The Mycenaean (my-suh-NEE-uhn) people arrived around 1600 B.C. They lived on the Greek mainland at the same time as the height of the Minoan civilization. The Mycenaeans were great traders and craftsmen. Although they had strong soldiers, foreign invaders (in-VADE-uhrz) threatened the Mycenaean kingdom around 1250 B.C. By the year 1000 B.C., the Mycenaean civilization had vanished.

Athens and Sparta

The men living in the city-states of Athens and Sparta left records about how they lived. Because of this, they are the two ancient Greek poleis we know the most about. Athens and Sparta had very different cultures.

Athens was at its height in the mid-fifth century B.C. It was a democratic city run by male citizens. Men were elected to their government positions. Athens placed a high value on personal qualities such as freedom, tolerance, and curiosity.

A	B	Γ	Δ	E	Z
Alpha	Beta	Gamma	Delta	Epsilon	Zeta
H	Θ	I	K	Λ	M
Eta	Theta	Iota	Kappa	Lambda	Mu
N	Ξ	O	Π	P	Σ
Ni	Xi	Omicron	Pi	Rho	Sigma
T	Y	Φ	X	Ψ	Ω
Tau	Upsilon	Phi	Chi	Psi	Omega

67

Sparta was a city led by military men and was not a democracy. All men had to serve in the military. Each boy belonged to the city-state at birth. In Sparta, discipline, loyalty, and self-denial were the most valuable traits a person could exhibit.

Greek Wars

The Greeks fought many wars. From about 492–447 B.C., they fought the Persians (PURR-zhuhnz). The Persians continuously attacked the Greeks. Finally, in a great victory, Athens' navy stopped them for good. But then, the city-states of Athens and Sparta turned on each other. They fought the Peloponnesian (PEL-uh-puh-NEE-shuhn) War from 431–404 B.C. The Spartans won, but both city-states were weakened.

In 334 B.C., the Greek leader Alexander the Great had a powerful army. He wanted to create the world's largest empire—and he did. The first civilization that his army conquered (KAHN-kuhrd) was Persia. Egypt was next. Then, he moved into Asia and conquered parts of the Indus Valley. He wanted to bring Greek culture to these places, so he had scientists, artists, and poets travel with his army. At one point, Alexander controlled a huge empire stretching from Greece to northern India.

Comprehension Question

Evaluate life in Athens and Sparta. In which city-state would you rather live and why?

#50083 — *Leveled Texts: World Cultures*

The Mighty Roman Empire

The City of Rome

Rome was founded around 753 B.C. How did it start? A story says that two brothers were raised by a wolf. Their names were Romulus (RAWM-yuh-luhs) and Remus (REE-muhs). One day, the brothers began building a city. The brothers fought. They each wanted the bigger part. Then, Romulus killed Remus. He became the king. He named the city Rome.

Rome had beautiful statues. It had great buildings. There was even a water system. It brought fresh water to the people. The Romans got some ideas from the Greeks. They used arches and columns in their bridges. The Romans had new ideas, too. They were the first to put domes on buildings. They made things that would last. You can see some of their buildings today.

Roman Rulers

Kings ruled early Rome. Then, the Roman Republic began in 509 B.C. It lasted almost 500 years. In this form of government, men picked senators. Then the senators ruled Rome. This group made the laws. The Roman men picked the men who would speak for them.

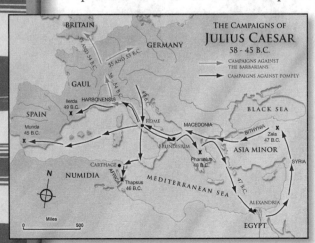

Julius Caesar (SEE-zuhr) was an army general. His troops liked him. Other people liked him, too. He won a big battle. Then, he made himself the head of Rome. He was in charge of the government. Many Romans felt that Caesar was acting like a king. They did not want a king. Some felt that he would end the Senate. So, a group of senators killed Caesar.

69

Caesar's son took charge. He was called Octavian. In 27 B.C., the Senate changed Octavian's name. He became Augustus (oh-GUHS-tuhs). He became Rome's first emperor. Augustus worked to improve the Roman Empire. He had the city streets cleaned. He had new buildings made. When Rome was very big, Trajan became the emperor.

Not all emperors did well. Caligula (kuh-LIG-yuh-luh) was Rome's third emperor. He went mad and was killed. Emperor Commodus (KAWM-uh-duhs) also went crazy. The Roman Republic had other problems, too. The Senate leaders argued. They did not agree on laws. Many Roman citizens had little say in their government. These common people were called plebeians (plih-BEE-uhnz). Unfair laws were passed. Plebeians rose up against the senators. They tried to force them to make changes.

Social Ranks

In Rome, a person was a citizen, a noncitizen, a plebeian, or a slave. Rich adult males were citizens. They voted. They owned land. They owned homes. All women and men from other places were noncitizens. Poor men were plebeians. They could vote. But, they could not speak in the Senate.

Slaves had no rights. Some were treated well. Others had to work long hours at hard jobs. Farmers needed slaves. They had to grow enough food to feed those who lived in the city.

Comprehension Question

Why did a group of senators kill Julius Caesar?

The Mighty Roman Empire

The Beautiful City of Rome

Rome was founded around 753 B.C. A myth says that a wolf raised two brothers. They were Romulus (RAWM-yuh-luhs) and Remus (REE-muhs). One day, they started making a city. The brothers fought. They each wanted the bigger part. Romulus killed Remus. He became the city's king. He named it Rome.

Rome had beautiful statues. It had great buildings. The Romans got ideas from the Greeks. They used arches and columns in their bridges. But, the Romans had new ideas, too. They were the first to put domes on buildings. Today, some of their buildings still stand.

Roman Rulers

Kings ruled early Rome. Then, Rome became a republic. Men chose its rulers. The Roman Republic began in 509 B.C. It lasted almost 500 years.

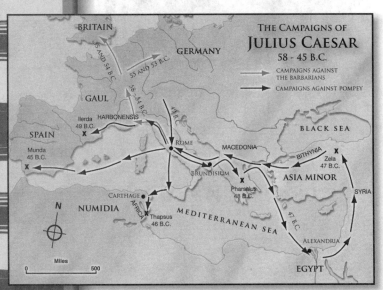

Julius Caesar (SEE-zuhr) was an army general. His troops liked him. And then, he won a big battle. So, he made himself the dictator of Rome. He took charge of the government. Many Romans felt that Caesar was acting like a king. They did not want a king. Some senators felt that he was a threat to them. In 44 B.C., a group of senators stabbed Caesar. He died.

71

Caesar's adopted son took over. He was called Octavian. In 27 B.C., the Senate changed Octavian's name. He became Augustus (oh-GUHS-tuhs). At the same time, he became Rome's first emperor. This was the start of the Roman Empire. Augustus worked to improve his empire. He cleaned the city streets. He had many new buildings put up. Later, Trajan was emperor when Rome reached its biggest size.

Not all emperors did well. Rome's third emperor was Caligula (kuh-LIG-yuh-luh). He went mad and was killed. Emperor Commodus (KAWM-uh-duhs) also went crazy in office. The Roman Republic had other problems, too. The Senate leaders fought among themselves. They did not agree on laws. Also, many of Rome's citizens had little say in their government. These people were called plebeians (plih-BEE-uhnz). They rose up against the senators. They tried to force them to make changes.

Social Ranks

In Rome, a person was a citizen, a noncitizen, a plebeian, or a slave. Rich adult males were citizens. They were the ones who voted and owned property. All women and men from other places were noncitizens. Poor men were plebeians. They could vote. But, they could not go to the Senate. So, laws were passed that were unfair to them.

Slaves had no rights. Most were born into slavery. Some were treated well by their owners. Others had to work long hours at hard jobs. Farmers needed slaves. They had to grow enough food to feed the Romans who lived in the city.

Comprehension Question

How did Julius Caesar affect life in Rome?

72

The Mighty Roman Empire

The Beautiful City of Rome

According to legend, Rome was founded around 753 B.C. A wolf raised two brothers. Their names were Romulus (RAWM-yuh-luhs) and Remus (REE-muhs). One day, the brothers decided to build parts of a city. They fought over the sizes of their territories, and Romulus killed Remus. Romulus became king of the city, which he named Rome.

Rome had beautiful statues and buildings. The Romans copied some architecture from ancient Greece. They used arches and columns in bridges and buildings. But, Romans had new ideas for buildings, too. They were the first people to use domes on buildings. Many of their buildings were so well constructed that they are still standing today.

Roman Rulers

Kings ruled early Rome. Then, Rome became a republic. This meant that its rulers were elected. The Roman Republic began in 509 B.C. and lasted almost 500 years.

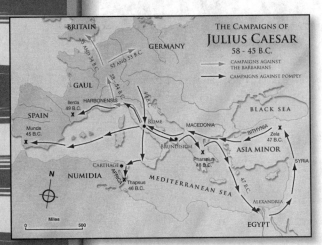

Julius Caesar (SEE-zuhr) was an important figure in the Roman Republic. He was a powerful army general well-liked by his troops. But then, after winning an important battle, he made himself Rome's dictator. This means that he took control of the government. Many Romans felt that Caesar was acting like a king. They did not want to go back to having kings. Some senators felt that he was a threat, and in 44 B.C., Caesar was assassinated (uh-SAS-suh-nate-ed). A group of senators stabbed him to death.

73

Caesar's heir (AIR) was his adopted son, Octavian. In 27 B.C., the Senate changed Octavian's name to Augustus (oh-GUHS-tuhs), and he became Rome's first emperor. This was the beginning of the Roman Empire. Augustus worked hard to strengthen his empire. He cleaned up the city streets and built many new buildings. Later, Trajan was emperor when Rome reached its greatest size.

Not all emperors were as successful. Caligula (kuh-LIG-yuh-luh) was Rome's third emperor. He went mad and was killed. Emperor Commodus (KAWM-uh-duhs) also went crazy while in office. The Roman Republic had other problems, too. The Senate leaders fought about laws. They disagreed on public affairs. Also, many of Rome's citizens had little say in their government. These common people were called plebeians (plih-BEE-uhnz). Unfair laws were passed, and they were frustrated. Then they revolted, or rose up, against the senators. They tried to force them to make changes.

Social Ranks

Romans were divided into citizens, noncitizens, plebeians, and slaves. Rich adult males were citizens. They could own property and vote. Women and men from other places were not citizens. Poor men were plebeians. They could vote. But they could not speak in the Senate.

Slaves had no rights. Many people were born into slavery. Some of them were treated well by their masters, while others had to work long hours at hard jobs. Farmers relied on slave labor to produce enough food to feed the Romans who dwelt in the city.

Comprehension Question

Why was Julius Caesar an important leader?

#50083 — Leveled Texts: World Cultures

The Mighty Roman Empire

The Beautiful City of Rome

According to legend, two brothers, Romulus (RAWM-yuh-luhs) and Remus (REE-muhs), had been raised by a wolf. One day, the brothers decided to build a magnificent city. However, when they fought over the size of their territories, Romulus murdered Remus. Romulus became king of the city, which he named Rome. This happened around 753 B.C.

Rome had beautiful statues and majestic buildings. The Romans copied designs such as arches and columns from Greece. The Romans also had new architectural ideas and were the first to use domes on buildings. Some of what they built is still standing today.

Rulers of Rome

Kings ruled early Rome. Then, Rome became a republic in 509 B.C. This meant that male citizens elected senators to serve in the Senate. These senators created Roman laws and made decisions for the Roman Republic. This form of government lasted almost 500 years.

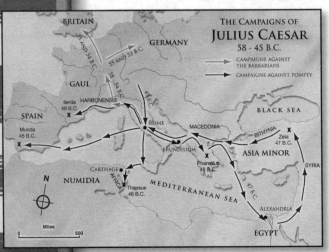

Julius Caesar (SEE-zuhr) was a powerful army general who was well-liked by his troops. But then, after winning an important battle, he made himself dictator and took charge of the government. Many Romans felt that Caesar was acting like a king, and they did not want to return to having kings. Some senators worried that Caesar would dismantle the Senate. They saw him as a threat, and in 44 B.C., a group of senators assassinated (uh-SAS-suh-nate-ed) Caesar.

75

Caesar's heir (AIR) was his adopted son, Gaius Octavius (GAY-uhs awk-TAY-vee-uhs), who went by the name Octavian. In 27 B.C., the Senate changed Octavian's name to Augustus (oh-GUHS-tuhs), and he became Rome's first emperor. Augustus worked to strengthen and improve the Roman Empire. He cleaned the city streets and had many new buildings erected. Later, Rome reached its greatest size under Emperor Trajan.

Not all emperors were successful. Caligula (kuh-LIG-yuh-luh), Rome's third emperor, went mad and was killed in office. Emperor Commodus (KAWM-uh-duhs) also went crazy. The Roman Republic had other problems as well. The senators often argued about laws and disagreed on public affairs. Also, many of Rome's citizens were commoners, or plebeians (plih-BEE-uhnz). They were frustrated by their lack of voice in the government because some of the laws hurt their interests. They eventually revolted in order to force the Senate to make changes.

Social Ranks

Romans were divided into citizens, noncitizens, plebeians, and slaves. Wealthy adult males were citizens. They could own property and vote. All women and foreigners were noncitizens. Poor men were plebeians. They could vote, but they could not speak in the Senate.

Slaves had no rights. Some of them were treated well by their masters. Others had to work long hours at difficult, dangerous, and dirty jobs. Farmers depended upon slave labor in order to produce enough food to feed the city's large population.

Comprehension Question

How did Julius Caesar's death affect life in Rome?

The Rise and Fall of the Roman Empire

A Strong Army

Soldiers made the Roman Empire strong. They were called legionnaires (lee-juh-NEARZ). Sometimes they fought to keep Rome in charge. At other times, they fought to win more land for Rome.

These troops used swords and knives. They wore metal armor. They had metal helmets. This helped to keep them safe. The army had to buy these things. It had to pay the men. This cost a lot of money. So, the Romans paid high taxes.

Roman Religion

Romans thought that the gods had great power. They thought the gods ran each person's life. The Romans did not want to make the gods angry. So they made sacrifices (SAK-ruh-fice-ez). This meant that they killed animals to make the gods happy. Then, there would be nice weather. They would have good crops. They would not go hungry.

Jupiter, Juno, and Minerva were important gods. The Romans built them temples. Jupiter was the sky god. He was the most important. His wife was Juno. She was the goddess of women. Their child was Minerva. She was a wise goddess. Romans saw their emperor as a god, too.

Romans wrote stories. These stories told how the gods and people got along. Some told why things happened. One story explained thunder. Another story told about the seasons.

The Romans did not mind most other faiths. But, they disliked Christianity. Christians did not believe in the Roman gods. This made the Romans mad. Then, in A.D. 64, a fire ruined most of the city of Rome. The emperor Nero said it was the Christians' fault. He made their faith against the law.

Many Christians were killed in awful ways. They died in front of big crowds. And, the people cheered! So Christians hid their faith. This went on for 200 years. Then, Emperor Constantine became a Christian. He wanted others to believe, too. After that, it was legal to be a Christian.

The Empire Falls but Lives On

The Roman Empire ended in A.D. 476. Its long borders made it hard to protect. Soldiers could not fight in different places at the same time. Their enemies knew this. So, they attacked in many places. The empire split in two. The Eastern Empire lasted 1,000 years longer than the Western Empire.

Romans influenced the world. Today, we use Roman numerals. Their laws are why we have some of today's laws. Their language was Latin. It is the basis for many languages used today. One is French. Some English words come from Latin, too.

Comprehension Question

Why did the Roman Empire fall?

#50083—*Leveled Texts: World Cultures*   © *Shell Education*

The Rise and Fall of the Roman Empire

A Strong Army

Legionnaires (lee-juh-NEARZ) made the Roman Empire strong. They were Rome's soldiers. Sometimes they fought to keep Rome in charge. At other times, they battled to win more land for Rome.

The army kept its men well-armed. They had swords and knives. The troops wore heavy metal armor and helmets. This helped keep the men from being killed. The army had to buy these things and pay the men. This cost lots of money, so the Romans paid high taxes.

Roman Religion

Romans thought that the gods had power over every part of their lives. They tried not to anger the gods. Early Romans honored the gods of nature. They made sacrifices (SAK-ruh-fice-ez). Often this meant that they killed animals. They thought this would make the gods happy. Then, they would have good weather and crops.

Jupiter, Juno, and Minerva were important gods. The Romans built temples in their honor. Jupiter, the sky god, was the highest. His wife, Juno, was the goddess of women. Their child was Minerva. She was the goddess of wisdom. Romans saw their emperor as a god, too.

79

#50083 — Leveled Texts: World Cultures

Romans wrote myths. These stories told about how the gods and people got along. These stories told about things in nature. Some told why things such as thunder and the seasons happened.

Romans let people practice other religions. But, they were against Christianity. Christians did not make sacrifices to the Roman gods. This made many Romans mad. Then, in A.D. 64, a fire ruined most of the city of Rome. Emperor Nero blamed the Christians. He said that they started the fire. He outlawed their faith.

Many Christians were killed in awful ways in front of cheering crowds. So, Christians had to hide their faith. This lasted for 200 years. Then, Emperor Constantine became a Christian. He praised Christianity. He gave back things that had been taken from the Christians. After that, it was legal to be a Christian.

The Empire Falls but Lives On

In spite of its brave troops, the Roman Empire ended in A.D. 476. Long borders made it hard to defend. Soldiers could not fight in lots of places at the same time. Their enemies knew this. So, they attacked in many places. The empire split into two parts. The Eastern Empire lasted 1,000 years longer than the Western Empire.

People around the world are still affected by the ancient Romans. We use Roman numerals. Their laws formed the basis of many modern laws. Latin, their language, is the basis for many languages. One is Spanish. Another is French. Some English words come from Latin, too.

Comprehension Question

For what reasons did the Roman Empire fall?

80

The Rise and Fall of the Roman Empire

A Strong Army

Legionnaires (lee-juh-NEARZ) gave the Roman Empire its strength. They were Rome's soldiers. Sometimes they fought to keep Rome in control in a region. At other times, they battled to win more land for Rome.

The army kept its men well-armed with swords and daggers. To guard against injuries, the men wore heavy armor and helmets. They had some of the best troops in the world. But, the army cost lots of money. The people had to pay high taxes to support it.

Roman Religion

Romans believed that the gods influenced every part of their lives. They always tried not to anger the gods. Early Romans worshipped the gods of nature. They made sacrifices (SAK-ruh-fice-ez) to make these gods happy. They thought that this would give them good weather and lots of crops.

The three most important gods were Jupiter, Juno, and Minerva. Jupiter, the sky god, was the supreme god. Juno, his wife, was the goddess of women. Their daughter, Minerva, was the goddess of wisdom. The Romans worshipped the gods at festivals and built temples in their honor. Romans believed that humans could have godlike qualities. They often worshipped emperors as gods.

81

Romans composed myths about how they interacted with the gods. Some of these myths explained the mysteries of the world, such as why thunder happens or the seasons change.

Romans were tolerant of other religions except for Christianity. Christians did not offer sacrifices to Roman gods. This made many Romans angry. To make matters worse, in A.D. 64, a great fire ruined most of the city of Rome. Nero, the emperor, blamed Christians for the fire. He outlawed their religion.

Many Christians were killed in horrible ways in front of cheering crowds. Christians had to worship in secret for 200 years. Then, Emperor Constantine became a Christian in A.D. 313. He urged others to convert and returned property that had been taken from Christians. Suddenly, it was good to be a Christian!

The Empire Falls but Lives On

Despite its brave legionnaires, the Roman Empire collapsed in A.D. 476. Its large size and its long borders made it easy to attack. The soldiers could not fight enemies in lots of places at the same time. Enemies attacked in many places. The borders crumbled. The empire was divided into two halves. The Eastern Empire lasted 1,000 years longer than the Western Empire.

People around the world are still influenced by ancient Roman culture. We use Roman numerals. Their laws formed the basis of modern legal systems. Latin, their language, is the basis for at least four languages, including Spanish and French. Some English words are based on Latin, too.

Comprehension Question

Describe the fall of the Roman Empire.

82

The Rise and Fall of the Roman Empire

A Strong Military

Legionnaires (lee-juh-NEARZ) gave the Roman Empire its strength. These soldiers fought to keep Rome in control of its vast holdings. They also battled to win more land for Rome.

The military kept these men well-armed with weapons such as swords and daggers. To prevent injuries, they wore heavy armor and helmets. The army's equipment and payroll were expensive. The Roman people paid high taxes to support it.

Roman Religion

Early Romans worshipped gods of nature. They made many animal sacrifices (SAK-ruh-fice-ez) to please the gods. They thought that this would give them good weather and a bountiful harvest. Romans believed that the gods had control over every part of their lives.

Jupiter, Juno, and Minerva were the three most important gods. Jupiter, the sky god, was the supreme god. Juno, his wife, was the goddess of women. Their daughter, Minerva, was the goddess of wisdom. The Romans built temples in their honor and worshipped them at festivals. Romans believed that humans could have godlike qualities and worshipped their emperors as gods.

© Shell Education   #50083—Leveled Texts: World Cultures

Romans composed myths about how they interacted with the gods. Some myths explained the mysteries in the natural world, such as the reason for thunder and the changing seasons.

Romans were tolerant of other religions except for Christianity. Christians refused to offer sacrifices to Roman gods, which made the Romans furious. To make matters worse, in A.D. 64, a massive fire almost destroyed the city of Rome. Nero, the emperor, blamed Christians for the fire and made their faith illegal.

Many Christians were killed in awful ways in front of large, cheering audiences. Persecuted Christians had to worship in secret for 200 years until A.D. 313. At that time Emperor Constantine became a Christian. He urged others to convert and returned property that had been seized from the Christians. Suddenly, it was good to be a Christian!

The Empire Falls but Lives On

Despite its brave legionnaires, the Roman Empire collapsed in A.D. 476. Its large size made it hard to govern all the people, and its long borders made it vulnerable to attack. The soldiers could not fight enemies in multiple places simultaneously. Rome's enemies continued attacking in many places to weaken the borders. Then, the empire divided into two halves. The Eastern Empire lasted 1,000 years longer than the Western Empire.

Today, people around the world are still influenced by ancient Roman culture. We use Roman numerals. Roman laws formed the basis of modern legislation. Their language, Latin, is the basis for at least four modern languages, including Spanish, Italian and French. Many English words are based on Latin roots.

Comprehension Question

How might the Romans have better protected their borders?

Early India

India is located between the East and the West. Over time, troops came from both sides. They took over the country. Each group that came to India changed it.

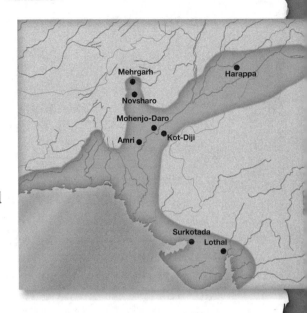

The first people to live there were the Dravidians (druh-VID-ee-uhnz). They settled in the southern and central parts of India. Some people who now live in southern India are their descendents (dih-SEN-duhntz). They can trace their families back to these people.

A second group came to the Indus Valley. They were called the Aryans (AH-ree-uhnz). They came from central Europe and Asia. They settled across northern India. Some of them moved around. They lived in tents. They took care of cattle. Others lived in towns. This caused most Dravidians to go south. But some of them stayed. The two groups of people started to take on each other's way of life.

The Aryans had a language. It was called Sanskrit (SAN-skrit). It is one of the oldest languages on Earth. It is part of a faith called Hinduism. This group set up a caste system, too. People were put into different groups based on importance. Priests were the most important. Soldiers were second. Next came farmers and other workers. Peasants and servants were at the bottom. People looked down on those who did not fit into a group. They were called untouchables.

Later, the Persian (PURR-zhuhn) King Darius (duh-RI-uhs) led an attack. He took over the Indus Valley and West Punjab (puhn-JAB). He ruled until he died. Then, his family ruled until the Greeks came. Alexander the Great overthrew them. But, his troops grew tired of fighting. And, the Indians fought back hard. The Greeks left India. India is one of the few places that did not fall to that strong army.

85

The Mauryan Empire

There was another kingdom in India before the Greeks came. It was the Mauryan (MOR-yuhn) Empire. It grew once the Greeks left. The people were located across most of northern India. This empire had a big army. It had a government. They also found a way to get taxes.

These leaders led easy lives. The poor people did not. The Mauryans ruled for about 140 years. Their strongest king was Ashoka (ah-SHOW-kuh). Under his rule, the empire took over most of India. This caused battles. When the king saw the battles, he got upset. He gave up war. He began to practice Buddhism. This faith was against hurting humans and animals.

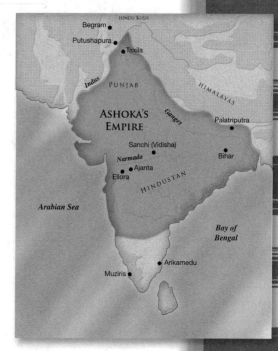

Ashoka wanted to teach others about Buddhism. He spread the faith through much of central Asia. Once he died, the Mauryan Empire began to fall apart. It was gone in less than 100 years.

Then, India split into hundreds of kingdoms. People came from outside India and gained control. They ruled central and northern India. Sometimes the kingdoms joined together. They fought to get rid of the invaders (in-VADE-uhrz). At other times, they fought against each other.

Comprehension Question

What is the caste system?

#50083— *Leveled Texts: World Cultures*

© *Shell Education*

Early India

India lies between the East and the West. Invaders (in-VADE-uhrz) came from both places. Each group that invaded India changed it in some way.

The first people were the Dravidians (druh-VID-ee-uhnz). They lived in the southern and central parts. Some people who now live in southern India are their descendents (dih-SEN-duhntz). They can trace their families back to these settlers.

A second group came to the Indus Valley. The Aryans (AH-ree-uhnz) were from central Europe and Asia. They lived in the Indus Valley for more than 1,000 years. They spread across northern India. Some of them moved around with their cattle. Others lived in villages and pushed the Dravidians south. Those who stayed started living like the Aryans. The Aryans took on some of the Dravidians' customs as well.

The Aryans came up with a language called Sanskrit (SAN-skrit). It is one of the world's oldest languages. It is part of Hinduism. They set up a caste system, too. It gave a status for each person. Priests were the most important. Soldiers were second. Next were merchants, farmers, and other workers. Peasants and servants were at the bottom. People looked down on those who did not fit into one of these groups. They were called untouchables.

Later, the Persian (PURR-zhuhn) King Darius (duh-RI-uhs) took over the Indus Valley and West Punjab (puhn-JAB). He ruled until he died. Then, his family ruled until the Greeks arrived. Alexander the Great overthrew them. But, the Indians fought back hard. And, Alexander's men were tired. So, the Greeks left India. It is one of the few places that did not completely fall to Alexander's strong army.

87

The Mauryan Empire

A kingdom began in northern India before the Greeks came. It was the Mauryan (MOR-yuhn) Empire. It grew once the Greeks left. These people spread across most of northern India. This empire had a big army. It had an organized government. It had a way to get taxes.

The leaders led easy lives. The peasants did not. The Mauryans ruled for about 140 years. Their strongest king was Ashoka (ah-SHOW-kuh). Under his rule, the empire took over most of India. This caused bloody battles. When the king saw the battles, he got upset. He gave up war. He began to practice Buddhism. This faith is against hurting humans and animals.

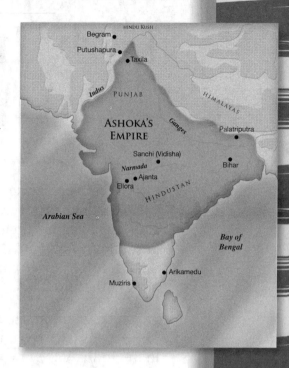

Ashoka wanted to teach others about Buddhism. He spread this faith through much of central Asia. When he died, the Mauryan Empire began to fall apart. It was gone in less than 100 years.

Then, India split into hundreds of kingdoms. Outsiders gained control. They ruled most of the central and northern parts. Sometimes these kingdoms banded together. They fought against common invaders. At other times, they fought among themselves.

Comprehension Question

Explain how the caste system worked.

#50083 — *Leveled Texts: World Cultures*

Early India

India lies between the East and the West. Its location makes it a natural place for invaders (in-VADE-uhrz) to attack. Each group that invaded the country changed it in some way.

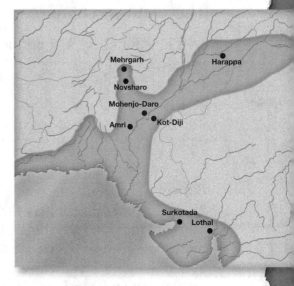

The earliest people, the Dravidians (druh-VID-ee-uhnz), lived in the southern and central parts of India. Some of their descendents (dih-SEN-duhntz) still live in southern India. This means that they can trace their families back to these settlers.

A second group of settlers, the Aryans (AH-ree-uhnz), came to the Indus Valley from central Europe and Asia. They lived in the Indus Valley for more than 1,000 years. The Aryans spread through northern India. Many of them wandered around tending cattle. Others settled in villages and pushed the Dravidian people farther south. Those who stayed started living like the Aryans. The Aryans took on some of the Dravidians' customs as well.

When the Aryans conquered (KAHN-kuhrd) the people of the Indus Valley, they created Sanskrit (SAN-skrit). It is the language of Hinduism. It is one of the world's oldest languages.

The Aryans also set up a caste system, which gave each person a set status. Priests were at the highest level. Soldiers were second. Next were merchants, farmers, and other workers. Peasants and servants were at the bottom. People looked down on those who did not fit into one of these groups. They were called untouchables.

Then, another invasion occurred. The Persian (PURR-zhuhn) King Darius (duh-RI-uhs) conquered the Indus Valley and West Punjab (puhn-JAB). His armies ruled both areas until he died. His family ruled until the Greeks arrived. Then, Alexander the Great overthrew them. But, Alexander's troops were tired. And, the Indians fought with great force. The Greeks left India. It is one of the few places that did not completely fall to Alexander's strong army.

89

The Mauryan Empire

A kingdom began in northern India before the Greeks invaded. This kingdom, the Mauryan (MOR-yuhn) Empire, grew once the Greeks left. These people spread across most of northern India. This empire had a big army. Its government was organized. It had a system to collect taxes.

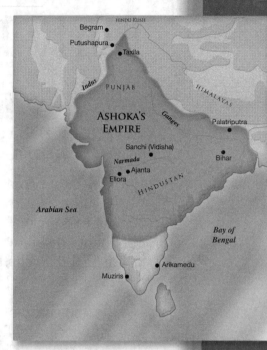

The leaders led comfortable lives. The peasants did not. The Mauryans ruled for about 140 years. Their strongest leader was King Ashoka (ah-SHOW-kuh). Under his rule, the Mauryan Empire took over almost all of India. This caused many bloody battles. When the king saw them, he was horrified. He gave up warfare and converted to Buddhism. This faith is against hurting humans and animals.

Ashoka wanted to teach his people about Buddhism. He spread this faith through much of central Asia. He insisted on nonviolence to humans and animals. Once he died, the Mauryan Empire began to fall apart. It was gone in less than 100 years.

India split into hundreds of small kingdoms. Foreign enemies seized control. They ruled most of central and northern India. Sometimes the kingdoms banded together to battle invaders. At other times, they fought among themselves.

Comprehension Question

How did the caste system affect people in India?

Early India

India lies between the East and the West, making it a natural place for invaders (in-VADE-uhrz) to attack. Invasions came from many places. Each group that overran the country changed it in some way.

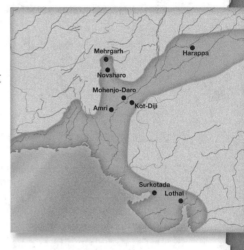

The earliest people, the Dravidians (druh-VID-ee-uhnz), lived in the south and central parts of India. The descendents (dih-SEN-duhntz) of these settlers still live in southern India. A second group of settlers, the Aryans (AH-ree-uhnz), came to the Indus Valley from central Europe and Asia. They lived in the Indus Valley for more than 1,000 years. The Aryans spread throughout northern India. Many of them wandered as nomads tending cattle. Some of them settled in villages, which pushed the Dravidian people farther south. The Dravidians who stayed started living like the Aryans. The Aryans took on some customs of the Dravidians as well.

After the Aryans conquered (KAHN-kuhrd) the Indus Valley, they developed a religion called Hinduism and Sanskrit (SAN-skrit), one of the world's oldest languages. They also instituted the caste system, which established the social status of people. Priests were at the highest level, followed by soldiers. Next were merchants, farmers, and craftsmen, while peasants and servants were at the bottom. Everyone looked down on the untouchables, who were people who did not fit into one of these groups.

An invasion occurred around 500 B.C. when King Darius (duh-RI-uhs) of Persia conquered the Indus Valley and West Punjab (puhn-JAB). His armies controlled these territories until he died. Then, his descendents ruled for 150 years until the Greek army of Alexander the Great overthrew them. However, India is one of the few places that did not completely fall to Alexander. His battle-weary men were exhausted, and the Indians fought back fiercely. The Greeks left India.

The Mauryan Empire

Before the Greek invasion, a kingdom had developed in northern India. This kingdom, the Mauryan (MOR-yuhn) Empire, grew once the Greeks left. The Mauryans spread across most of northern India. This empire's first leader had a huge army and a well-organized government with a system of tax collection.

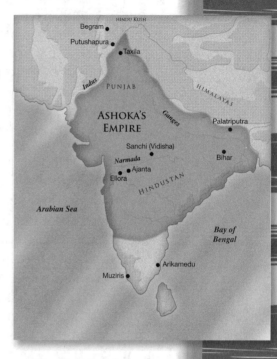

The leaders led comfortable lives. However, life for the peasants was difficult and demanding. The Mauryans ruled for about 140 years (321–185 B.C.). The empire reached its height under King Ashoka (ah-SHOW-kuh). He was the empire's last great ruler. While he was king, the Mauryan Empire seized control of almost all of India. This caused many terrible, bloody battles. Ashoka, horrified by the slaughter he saw, gave up warfare. He converted to Buddhism, a religion against any violence done to humans or animals.

Ashoka wanted to teach his people about Buddhism. He brought this religion to much of central Asia. After he died, the Mauryan Empire collapsed in less than 100 years.

Northern India split into hundreds of separate and divided kingdoms. Foreign enemies seized control and ruled most of central and northern India. Sometimes the kingdoms banded together against a common enemy from the north, while at other times, they battled among themselves.

Comprehension Question

How did the caste system impact people in India?

#50083— Leveled Texts: World Cultures

Indian Rulers

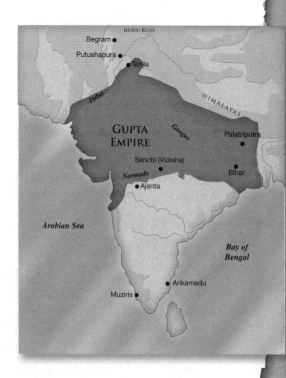

The Gupta Empire

King Chandra Gupta I (chuhn-DRUH GOOP-tuh the first) brought northern India together. He set up a new empire. His son had the same name. He loved art and science. While the son ruled, great works of art were made. People learned new things about science. This was called the "golden age."

Then the Gupta Empire ended. India broke apart. Small Hindu kingdoms formed. These groups fought against each other. There were wars for the next 1,000 years.

The Mughal Empire

Muslims (MUHZ-luhmz) are people who believe in Islam (is-LAWM). A man named Muhammad (moo-HAM-uhd) began this faith. The Muslims came into India. They took more and more land. By 1526, they ruled much of India. They began the Mughal (MUH-guhl) Empire. They built mosques, or temples. These temples had domes and towers.

Most Mughal leaders wanted the people to follow Islam. Yet, most Hindus kept their faith. Then, the last ruler wanted all Hindus to be Muslims. He tried to force them to do that. They fought against him. This hurt the empire. The Mughal Empire ended by 1800.

Great Britain Takes Control

Great Britain came to India. It set up the East India Company. The British chose its leaders. The Company held power over half of India. Indian princes owned the other half. These princes agreed not to fight the British.

The British made changes. Some changes helped the Indians. Others hurt them. The Indians were not happy. They did not like British rule.

93

Indian troops were part of the British army. A rumor spread. It said that the British bullets were covered with animal fat. Some said that it was pig fat. Others said that it was cow fat. Muslims think that pigs are dirty. Hindus think cows are holy. People of both faiths got angry. They turned against the British. They started fighting. When it was over, the East India Company had ended. Yet, the British were still in control of India.

Freedom

The Indians wanted to be in charge of their country. They wanted to rule themselves. The British talked about letting them do so. But then they passed new laws. These laws cut back on their rights!

Mohandas Gandhi (mo-HAWN-duhs GAWN-dee) was a Hindu lawyer. He spent his life working for India's freedom. But, he did not use weapons. He did not use force. He used protests. He taught his people that they could disobey without hurting the British. He gave speeches. He held marches.

The British put Gandhi in jail. Still, he would not use force. His protests took time. But they worked. India gained its freedom in 1947.

Comprehension Question

How did Gandhi help his people?

#50083— *Leveled Texts: World Cultures*   © *Shell Education*

Indian Rulers

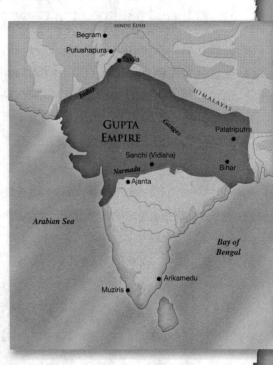

The Gupta Empire

King Chandra Gupta I (chuhn-DRUH GOOP-tuh the first) brought together all of northern India. He set up the Gupta Empire. His son wanted people to love art and science. While his son ruled, works of art were made. People learned new things about science. This peaceful time is called the "golden age."

The Gupta Empire lasted until around A.D. 550. Then it ended. India broke apart. Many small Hindu kingdoms formed. Wars were fought on and off for the next 1,000 years.

The Mughal Empire

Muslims (MUHZ-luhmz) are people who believe in Islam (is-LAWM). A man named Muhammad (moo-HAM-uhd) began this faith. He started it around A.D. 600. The Muslims invaded India more than once. By 1526, they held much of India. They began the Mughal (MUH-guhl) Empire. The Mughals built beautiful mosques. These domed temples had towers. The greatest Mughal leader was Akbar (AK-buhr). He built the Taj Mahal.

Most Mughal leaders wanted the people to follow Islam. Yet many Hindus kept their faith. Then, the last ruler tried to make all Hindus be Muslims. This caused fighting. It made the empire weak. The Mughal Empire was over by 1800.

Great Britain Takes Control

Great Britain moved into India. It set up the East India Company. The British chose its leaders. The East India Company had power over half of India. Indian princes owned the other half. But these princes agreed not to fight Great Britain.

The British made changes. Some changes helped the Indians. Others hurt the people. The Indians were not happy. They did not like British rule.

95

In 1857, Indian troops were part of the British army. A rumor spread. It said that their bullets were coated with animal fat. Some said it was pig fat. Others said it was cow fat. Muslims think that pigs are unclean. Hindus think cows are holy. Both Muslims and Hindus got upset. They felt insulted. The Indian troops turned against the British. They started fighting. When it was over, the East India Company had ended. Yet, the British government still had control of India.

Freedom

The Indians wanted to rule themselves. The British talked about giving them control. At the same time, they passed new laws. These laws reduced their rights!

Mohandas Gandhi (mo-HAWN-duhs GAWN-dee) was a lawyer. He came from a rich Hindu family. He spent his life working for India's freedom. He used nonviolent protests. He taught his people that they could disobey without hurting the British or their property. He gave speeches. He held marches. The British put him in jail. Still, he would not use force to get freedom. His methods took time. But in the end, they worked. On August 15, 1947, India gained its freedom.

Comprehension Question

What did Gandhi try to teach his people?

Indian Rulers

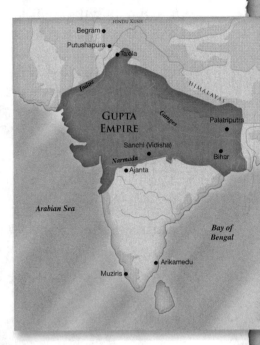

The Gupta Empire

King Chandra Gupta I (chuhn-DRUH GOOP-tuh) set up the Gupta Empire. He brought together the whole northern part of India. This empire reached its peak under his son. Chandra Gupta II wanted his people to study art and science. Many scientific gains were made during his reign. This peaceful, stable time is called the "golden age."

The Gupta Empire lasted until around A.D. 550. After it ended, India broke apart again. It became many separate Hindu kingdoms. Great conflict occurred during the next 1,000 years.

The Mughal Empire

Muslims (MUHZ-luhmz) are people who believe in Islam (is-LAWM). The prophet named Muhammad (moo-HAM-uhd) began this religion around A.D. 600. The Muslims invaded India several times between 1000 and 1500. By 1526, much of India was under Muslim control. They began the Mughal (MUH-guhl) Empire. The Mughals built some of the world's most beautiful mosques. These domed temples had towers. The greatest Mughal leader, Akbar (AK-buhr), built the Taj Mahal.

Most rulers wanted everyone to follow Islam. Still, many Hindus kept their religion. Then, the last Mughal ruler tried to force the Hindus to be Muslims. This caused a revolt. It weakened the empire. The Mughal Empire had ended by the turn of the 19th century (1800).

Great Britain Takes Control

Next, Great Britain moved into India. It set up a company called the East India Company. Leaders chosen by the British government ruled this company. The East India Company controlled about half of India. Indian princes controlled the other half. These princes pledged their loyalty to Great Britain.

The British made changes. Some changes helped the Indians. Others hurt the people. They were unhappy under British rule.

97

In 1857, a rumor spread among Indian soldiers serving in the British army. It said that their bullets had been greased with animal fat. Some said it was pig fat. Others said it was cow fat. The Islam religion says that pigs are unclean. Hindus think cows are holy. So, both Muslims and Hindus felt insulted. The Indian soldiers turned against the British. When the fighting ceased, the East India Company had ended. Yet, the British government kept control of India.

Independence

The Indians wanted to rule themselves. The British talked about giving them control. At the same time, they passed new laws. These laws reduced the Indians' rights!

Mohandas Gandhi (mo-HAWN-duhs GAWN-dee) was a lawyer. He came from a rich Hindu family. He spent his life working for India's freedom. He used nonviolent protests. Gandhi taught his people that they could disobey without hurting the British or their property. He gave speeches and held marches. The British put him in prison. Still, he would not use violence to gain freedom. His methods took time, but in the end they worked. On August 15, 1947, India received its independence.

Comprehension Question

What methods did Gandhi use to gain freedom for his people?

#50083— Leveled Texts: World Cultures

Indian Rulers

The Gupta Empire

In A.D. 319, King Chandra Gupta I (chuhn-DRUH GOOP-tuh) set up the Gupta Empire and brought together the entire northern part of India. This empire reached its peak under his son, Chandra Gupta II, who encouraged his people to study art and science. Many scientific gains were made during his reign, a peaceful, stable time known as the "golden age."

The Gupta Empire lasted until around A.D. 550. After it ended, India broke apart into many separate Hindu kingdoms. Great conflict occurred during the next millennium (1,000 years).

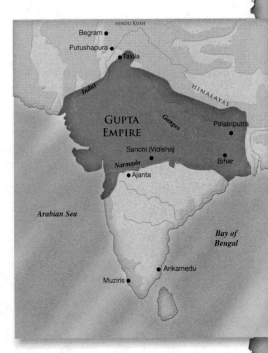

The Mughal Empire

Muslims (MUHZ-luhmz) are people who believe in the Islam (is-LAWM) religion. A prophet named Muhammad (moo-HAM-uhd) began this religion around A.D. 600. The Muslims invaded India several times between 1000 and 1500. By 1526, much of India was under Muslim control, and they began the Mughal (MUH-guhl) Empire. The Mughals built some of the world's most beautiful mosques. These domed temples had towers. The greatest Mughal leader, Akbar (AK-buhr), built the Taj Mahal.

Most Mughal leaders wanted everyone to follow Islam's beliefs and rules. Still, many Hindus kept their religion. Then, the last ruler tried to force all of the Hindus to become Muslims. This caused a revolt that seriously weakened the empire. It was over by the turn of the 19th century (1800).

Great Britain Takes Control

In the early 1800s, Great Britain moved into India and established the East India Company. Leaders chosen by the British government ruled the East India Company, which controlled about half of India. Indian princes controlled the other half. In return for keeping this control, they pledged their loyalty to Great Britain.

The British caused many changes in India. Some of these changes benefited the Indians, while others hurt the people. The Indians were unhappy under British rule.

99

In 1857, a rumor spread among Indian soldiers serving in the British army that their bullets had been greased with animal fat. Some said it was pig fat, and others said it was cow fat. Muslims believe that pigs are unclean, and Hindus consider cows holy. Thus, both Muslims and Hindus were offended. The Indian soldiers turned against the British in a revolt that destroyed the East India Company. Yet, the British government retained control of India.

Independence

The Indians wanted to rule themselves. The British talked about giving Indians control while at the same time passing laws that diminished their rights!

Mohandas Gandhi (mo-HAWN-duhs GAWN-dee) was a lawyer from a wealthy Hindu family who dedicated his life to achieving India's freedom. He used nonviolent protests such as speeches and marches. The British imprisoned him. Still, he refused to resort to violence. His methods took time, but eventually they worked. On August 15, 1947, India received its independence.

Comprehension Question

How did Gandhi set an example for the people of India?

100

Ancient China

The first settlers of China lived in the Yellow River Valley. The farmers grew crops. Men made silk. They used clay to make dishes and pots. Mountains along the borders kept them apart from other nations. So, there was not much trade.

The first culture was under the Xia (she-AH) dynasty (DIE-nuhs-tee). A dynasty is one family. It holds all the power in a nation. The Xia ruled for 400 years.

The Shang Dynasty

The Shang dynasty came next. It ruled for 600 years. The Shang people worked with bronze. They made tools and wheels.

The oldest Chinese writings come from the Shang. The people carved words on animal shells and bones. These are called oracle (OR-uh-kuhl) bones.

Long-Lasting Zhou Dynasty

Then, the Zhou (JO) dynasty took charge. It lasted for 900 years. Near its end the rulers became weak. They could not keep control of their land. Small states broke away. Their troops fought each other. Wars broke out. Thousands of men died. These battles ruined farms and towns.

Confucius (kuhn-FYOO-shuhs) lived during this time. He thought about the meaning of life. He said that family was most important. He taught that a person should be honest and work hard. He also said that a person must follow rules.

101

Short but Sweet: The Qin Dynasty

The Qin (CHIN) dynasty lasted only 15 years. Yet Emperor Qin Shi Huang (CHIN SHE HWANG) did a lot during this time. First, he stopped the battles. He took charge of all of China. He formed one government.

Other leaders had built walls to keep their areas safe. Emperor Qin chose to join these walls. This was the start of what would become the Great Wall of China. Qin set standard weights and measures. He made writing better. He had roads and canals made. He was a man who got things done.

Emperor Qin wanted a great tomb. This tomb would show his power. He had artists make over 7,000 life-sized men. They made these soldiers from red clay. This clay is called terra-cotta (tear-ruh-KAWT-tuh). When Qin died, these troops stood guard over him.

The Han Dynasty

Emperor Qin died. His sons lost control of China. The Han (HAWN) dynasty took over. It lasted more than 400 years. By then, China was the biggest country in the world. It had 60 million people. The Han built a trade route. It was called the Silk Road. It went from China to Europe. For the first time there was a road between Asia and Europe.

Land under the rule of the Han Dynasty

Current boundaries of China and Mongolia

HAN

Then the Han rule ended. Wars broke out. Barbarians (bawr-BER-ee-uhnz) took over northern China. These people had no culture (art or writing). Many rulers held parts of southern China.

Comprehension Question

What is a dynasty?

#50083 — *Leveled Texts: World Cultures*

Ancient China

The first Chinese settled in the Yellow River Valley. The farmers grew crops. Craftsmen made silk and clay dishes and pots. The mountains along China's border kept it apart from other nations. So there was not much trade.

The first society was the Xia (she-AH) dynasty (DIE-nuhs-tee). A dynasty is one family that holds the power in a nation. The Xia ruled for 400 years.

The Shang Dynasty

The Shang dynasty held power for nearly 600 years. Its people used bronze. They made tools and wheels. The oldest Chinese writings come from this time. The people carved words on animal shells and bones. These are called oracle (OR-uh-kuhl) bones.

Long-Lasting Zhou Dynasty

Next, the Zhou (JO) dynasty ruled for 900 years. But near the end of this time, the emperors grew weak. They could not keep control. Small states broke away. Their troops fought each other. Soon civil war began. Thousands of men died. Bloody battles ruined farms and towns.

Confucius (kuhn-FYOO-shuhs) lived during this time. He was a philosopher. He thought about life and its meaning. He said that family was most important. He taught that it was a person's duty to be honest, work hard, and follow rules.

103

Short but Sweet: The Qin Dynasty

The Qin (CHIN) dynasty lasted only about 15 years. Yet, Emperor Qin Shi Huang (CHIN SHE HWANG) did a lot in this time. First, he stopped the battles. He took control of all of China.

Over the years, other leaders had built walls to keep their areas safe. Emperor Qin decided to join these walls. This was the start of what became the Great Wall of China.

Qin set standard weights and measures. He made written language the same for all of China. To connect towns, he had roads made and canals dug. He formed a central government.

Emperor Qin wanted a fancy tomb. He wanted it to show his power and importance. So, he had artists make over 7,000 life-sized terra-cotta (tear-ruh-KAWT-tuh) (red clay) troops. After Quin died, they stood guard over his tomb.

The Han Dynasty

Emperor Qin died. His sons lost control of China. The Han (HAWN) dynasty took over. It lasted more than 400 years. At this time, China was the world's biggest country. It had about 60 million people. The Han built a trade route from China to Europe. This great Silk Road was the first link between Asia and Europe.

Then the Han dynasty fell apart. Wars broke out. Barbarians (bawr-BER-ee-uhnz) took control of the northern part of China. These people had no culture (art or writing). Other rulers held parts of southern China.

Comprehension Question

Describe one dynasty.

#50083—*Leveled Texts: World Cultures*

Ancient China

The first Chinese settled in the Yellow River Valley. They were farmers and craftsmen. In addition to crops, they made pottery and silk. The first society was the Xia (she-AH) dynasty (DIE-nuhs-tee). A dynasty is one family that holds the power in a nation. The Xia ruled from about 2000 to 1600 B.C. The mountains along China's border kept it separate from other nations, so there was not a lot of trade during this time.

The Shang Dynasty

The Shang dynasty held power from around 1600 to 1046 B.C. Its people used bronze to make tools and wheels. The oldest Chinese writings come from this time. The people carved words on animal shells and bones. These are called oracle (OR-uh-kuhl) bones.

Long-Lasting Zhou Dynasty

Next, the Zhou (JO) dynasty reigned for 900 years. This dynasty kept written records of what happened on a daily basis. The final Zhou emperors were weak and could not control the people. Many small states broke away. The armies of these states fought one another. Soon civil war erupted. Thousands of men died in bloody battles. The countryside was destroyed.

At this time, Confucius (kuhn-FYOO-shuhs) was a philosopher. Philosophers want to understand life and its meaning. He said that family was of top importance. He taught that it was necessary to be honest, work hard, and obey rules.

Short but Sweet: The Qin Dynasty

The Qin (CHIN) dynasty came after the fall of the Zhou. It only lasted about 15 years. Yet Emperor Qin Shi Huang (CHIN SHE HWANG) accomplished much in this short time. He ended the constant battling and unified the nation. Qin took control of all of China.

Over the years, other leaders had built walls to protect their territories. Qin decided to join these walls and make them longer. This was the start of what became the Great Wall of China.

Qin set standard weights and measures. He made written language more uniform. To connect towns, he had roads and canals constructed. He formed a centralized government.

Qin wanted a tomb to display his power and importance. He had artists create over 7,000 life-sized terra-cotta (tear-ruh-KAWT-tuh) (red clay) soldiers. These soldiers had wooden weapons. After Qin died, they stood guard over his tomb.

The Han Dynasty

When Qin died, his sons lost control of the country. The Han (HAWN) dynasty began. Lasting more than 400 years, it was one of the strongest in Chinese history. During this time, China had a population of 60 million people, which made it the world's largest country. The great Silk Road, a trade route from China to Europe, was finished during this time. It was the first link between Asia and European nations.

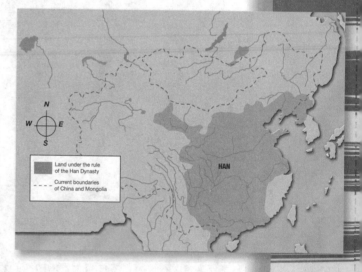

Land under the rule of the Han Dynasty

Current boundaries of China and Mongolia

HAN

Once the Han dynasty crumbled, wars followed. Barbarians (bawr-BER-ee-uhnz) controlled the northern part of China. These people had no culture. Different rulers controlled parts of southern China.

Comprehension Question

Compare and contrast two dynasties.

Ancient China

The first Chinese settled in the Yellow River Valley. They were farmers and craftsmen. In addition to crops, they produced pottery and silk. The mountains along China's border kept it separate from other civilizations (siv-uh-luh-ZAY-shuhnz), so there was little trade during this time.

When one family holds all the power in a nation, it is called a dynasty (DIE-nuhs-tee). The first society was the Xia (she-AH) dynasty, which lasted from about 2000 to 1600 B.C.

The Shang Dynasty

The Shang dynasty reigned from around 1600 to 1046 B.C. Its people used bronze to make tools and wheels. They also produced the oldest Chinese writings ever found. The people left records by carving words on animal shells and bones called oracle (OR-uh-kuhl) bones.

Long-Lasting Zhou Dynasty

The Zhou (JO) dynasty reigned for 900 years—the longest dynasty in Chinese history. This dynasty kept extensive written records. The late Zhou emperors grew weak and could not control the people. Smaller states broke away, and their armies fought against each other. Soon civil war erupted, and thousands of men perished in bloody battles. The Chinese countryside was destroyed.

During this time a man named Confucius (kuhn-FYOO-shuhs) was a philosopher who wanted to understand existence and its meaning. He believed that family was of supreme importance. Confucius taught that everyone should be honest, work hard, and obey rules.

107

Short but Sweet: The Qin Dynasty

The Qin (CHIN) dynasty gained power after the Zhou's fall. Their reign only lasted about 15 years, yet Emperor Qin Shi Huang (CHIN SHE HWANG) accomplished much in this time. He ended the constant battling by unifying the nation. Qin took control of all of China. He formed a centralized government.

Over the years, other leaders had built walls to protect their territories. Emperor Qin decided to join these walls and make them longer, forming the basis of what became the Great Wall of China. Emperor Qin established standard weights and measures and made written language uniform. To connect towns, he had roads and canals constructed.

Qin wanted a magnificent tomb that displayed his power and significance. Thus, he had artists create over 7,000 life-sized terra-cotta (tear-ruh-KAWT-tuh) (red clay) warriors to stand guard over his tomb.

Land under the rule of the Han Dynasty

Current boundaries of China and Mongolia

HAN

Prosperous Han Dynasty

After Qin died, his sons lost control. The Han (HAWN) dynasty took over. It lasted from 206 B.C. to A.D. 220 and was one of the strongest in Chinese history. During the Han reign, China was the largest country in the world, with a population of 60 million. The great Silk Road, a trade route forming the first link between Asian and European nations, was completed during this time.

Once the powerful Han dynasty crumbled, wars occurred. Barbarians (bawr-BER-ee-uhnz), uncivilized people who had no culture, seized control of the northern part of China. Different rulers controlled parts of southern China.

Comprehension Question

How did the dynasties impact Chinese history?

108

More Chinese History

China was brought back together by the Sui (SWAY) dynasty (DIE-nuhs-tee). They built new bridges. Some bridges hung in the air. Huge iron chains held them up. These bridges made it easier to move around. People could cross wide rivers.

About 1,300 years ago, the Chinese started to print. This began under the Tang (TAWNG) dynasty. They carved blocks of wood. They put ink on them. Then, they pressed the blocks on paper. They also painted on silk scrolls.

Next came the Song (SOUNG) dynasty. At this time, the Chinese made the first compass. They made the first paper money, too.

The Mongols Take Over

The Mongols (MAWN-guhlz) came into China. They took over. They were in charge for almost 100 years. They took over parts of Europe as well. So people traveled to and from China. The things that the Chinese had invented spread to other parts of the world.

Genghis Khan (jen-guhs-KAWN) was a Mongol. He began the Yuan (YWAWN) dynasty. He was the first man to rule China who was not Chinese. He ruled the biggest land empire ever. He supported more trade between Europe and China.

The Ming Dynasty

Zhu Yuanzhang (JOO you-AHN-jahng) led a revolt. He took power away from the Mongols. He was the first emperor of the Ming dynasty. This dynasty built a lot of ships. It had a big navy.

The Ming dynasty also built the Forbidden City. Tall red walls went around the city. It had a wide moat. This was a ditch full of water that went around the walls. The emperor and his family lived inside the city. Common people could not go in.

The End of the Chinese Dynasties

The Manchu (MAN-choo) dynasty was the last dynasty of China. It held power for more than 250 years. During this time, China gained more land.

People from Europe traded with China. But there was only one port open for trade. China did not buy many goods. The people from Europe did not like this. They wanted to trade more. So, the Treaty of Nanking made China open more ports. Forced trading was bad for China. It hurt their economy. This made people mad. It led to the Taiping Rebellion (TIE-ping rih-BEL-yuhn). In a rebellion, armed people fight against their leader. More revolts followed. These fights ended the Chinese dynasties.

Modern China

In 1912, the Republic of China was founded. There were two strong groups. They had different ideas. One group was the Nationalist Party. It wanted people to be in charge of their own lives. The other group was the Communist Party. It wanted the government to control everything.

In 1934, the Nationalists fought the Communists. The Communists won. They took charge. They formed The People's Republic of China. They rule China today.

Comprehension Question

Why did China have just one port?

More Chinese History

China was reunited during the Sui (SWAY) dynasty (DIE-nuhs-tee). New kinds of bridges were built. Some of these bridges hung in the air. Huge iron chains held them up. This let people cross wide rivers. It made moving around easier.

About 1,300 years ago, the Chinese started to print. They carved wooden blocks. They inked them. Then, they pressed the blocks on paper. They painted on silk scrolls. This occurred under the Tang (TAWNG) dynasty.

Next came the Song (SOUNG) dynasty. During this time, the Chinese made the first compass. They made the first paper money.

The Mongols Take Over

The Mongols (MAWN-guhlz) took control of China. They were in charge for almost 100 years. They held much of Eastern Europe, too. During this time, people traveled to and from China. People from many lands visited the country.

Genghis Khan (jen-guhs-KAWN) began the Yuan (YWAWN) dynasty. He was the first man to rule China who was not Chinese. He held the largest land empire ever. He supported more trade between Europe and China.

The Ming Dynasty

Zhu Yuanzhang (JOO you-AHN-jahng) led a revolt. He took power away from the Mongols. He was the first emperor of the Ming dynasty. This dynasty built a big navy.

The Ming dynasty also built the Forbidden City. Tall red walls and a wide moat surrounded it. The moat was a ditch filled with water. The emperor and his family lived inside the city. Common people could not go in.

The End of the Chinese Dynasties

China's last dynasty was the Manchu (MAN-choo). It held power for more than 250 years. During this time, China grew even larger.

People from Europe traded with China. But just one port was open for trade. The Chinese did not buy many goods. The people from Europe did not like such limited trade. The Treaty of Nanking made China open more ports. The forced trading hurt the Chinese economy. This led to the Taiping Rebellion (TIE-ping rih-BEL-yuhn). In a rebellion, people rise up against their government. More revolts followed. The Chinese dynasties were over.

Modern China

In 1912, the Republic of China was founded. There were two strong groups in the nation. They had different ideas. The Nationalist Party said that people should be in charge of their own lives. The other group was the Communist Party. It said that the government should control everything.

In 1934, the Nationalists fought the Communists. The Communists won. They took over mainland China. They formed The People's Republic of China. They still rule China today.

Comprehension Question

Why did China open more ports for trading?

#50083— *Leveled Texts: World Cultures*

More Chinese History

China was reunited under the Sui (SWAY) dynasty (DIE-nuhs-tee) (A.D. 581–618). During this reign, suspension (suh-SPEN-shuhn) bridges were built. Such bridges hung in the air, held up by huge iron chains. This made it easier to cross wide rivers.

More achievements occurred during the Tang (TAWNG) dynasty (A.D. 618–907). Around A.D. 700, the Chinese started to print. They carved wooden blocks and inked them. Then, the damp blocks were pressed against paper. They created beautiful pictures painted on silk scrolls, too.

Next, came the Song (SOUNG) dynasty. During this time China invented the compass and paper money.

The Mongols Conquer China

The Mongol (MAWN-guhl) invaders (in-VADE-uhrz) attacked after the fall of the Song dynasty. They had control of China from A.D. 1279 to 1368. The Mongols held much of Eastern Europe, too. So, during this time, people from many places traveled to and from China.

A man named Genghis Khan (jen-guhs-KAWN) began the Yuan (YWAWN) dynasty. Khan was the first man to rule China who was not Chinese. He ruled the largest land empire in history. He encouraged trade between Europe and China.

#50083—Leveled Texts: World Cultures

The Ming Dynasty

Zhu Yuanzhang (JOO you-AHN-jahng) led a revolt. He overthrew the Mongols. Then, he became the first emperor of the Ming dynasty. This dynasty created a large navy.

The Forbidden City was built during this reign. It took more than 10 years to erect. Surrounded by a wide moat and high walls, the Chinese emperor and his family lived within the city. Common people could not enter its red walls.

The End of the Chinese Dynasties

China's last dynasty, the Manchu (MAN-choo), held power from 1644 to 1911. During this era, China expanded its borders. Europeans traded with China. But there was just one port open for trading. The Chinese did not import many goods. The Europeans disliked such limited trade with China. The Treaty of Nanking forced China to open more ports. The forced trading damaged the Chinese economy. Soon, the Taiping Rebellion (TIE-ping rih-BEL-yuhn) took place. A rebellion is an armed fight against the government. More rebellions followed. These battles ended the Chinese dynasties.

Modern China

In 1912, the Republic of China was founded. The two most powerful groups in the nation had different ideas. The Nationalist Party wanted to unify China. This group believed that people should have control over their lives. The other group was the Communist Party. They wanted the government to control everything.

In 1934, the Nationalists fought the Communists. The Communists won and took over mainland China. They formed The People's Republic of China. This government leads China today.

Comprehension Question

What happened when China opened more ports for trading?

More Chinese History

China was reunited under the Sui (SWAY) dynasty (DIE-nuhs-tee) (A.D. 581–618). During this reign, transportation advances were made. For example, to make it easier to cross wide rivers, long suspension (suh-SPEN-shuhn) bridges were constructed. Such bridges hung in the air, supported by enormous iron chains.

Other achievements occurred during the Tang (TAWNG) dynasty (A.D. 618–907). Around A.D. 700, the Chinese started printing by carving wooden block, inking them, and then pressing the damp blocks against paper scrolls. They also created beautiful paintings on silk scrolls.

Next came the Song (SOUNG) dynasty. During this time, China invented the compass and paper money.

The Mongols Conquer China

The Mongol (MAWN-guhl) invaders (in-VADE-uhrz) attacked after the fall of the Song dynasty. They had control of China from A.D. 1279 to 1368. The Mongols held much of Eastern Europe as well. During this time, people from many places journeyed to and from China.

A man named Genghis Khan (jen-guhs-KAWN) began the Yuan (YWAWN) dynasty. Khan was the first man to rule China who was not Chinese. He ruled the largest land empire in history and encouraged trade between Europe and China.

115

The Ming Dynasty

Zhu Yuanzhang (JOO you-AHN-jahng) led a revolt that overthrew the Mongol rulers and established himself as the first emperor of the Ming dynasty. This dynasty created an impressive navy.

The Forbidden City was constructed during this reign. It took more than a decade to erect. Surrounded by a wide moat and high walls, the Chinese emperor and his family lived within the city. Common people could not enter its red walls.

The End of the Chinese Dynasties

China's last dynasty, the Manchu (MAN-choo), held power from 1644 to 1911. During this time, China expanded its borders. Europeans traded with China, but there was only one port open for trading. The Chinese did not import many goods and the Europeans disliked such limited trade with China. The Treaty of Nanking forced China to open more ports. However, the forced trading damaged the Chinese economy, and the Taiping Rebellion (TIE-ping rih-BEL-yuhn) occurred. A rebellion is an armed fight against the government. More rebellions followed. These battles eliminated the Chinese dynasties.

Modern China

In 1912, the Republic of China was founded. The two most powerful groups in the nation had different ideas. The Nationalist Party believed that people should have control over their lives. The other group, the Communist Party, wanted the government to control everything.

In 1934, the Nationalists fought the Communists. The victorious Communists took over mainland China and formed The People's Republic of China. This government leads China today.

Comprehension Question

How do you think opening China's ports affected the world?

African History

Africa is very big. It is bigger than the United States and Europe put together. Africa is located south of Europe. It is southwest of the Middle East.

Long ago, Africans made a lot of money through trade. Groups of people owned trade routes. A route is a path or a road. They made people pay fees to use their roads. People needed the roads to trade with others far away. This gave power to the owners of trade routes. When they lost control of these routes, they lost their power.

The Kush and the Kingdom of Aksum

The Kush (KUHSH) were one of the first civilizations (siv-uh-luh-ZAY-shuhnz). They ruled what is now Sudan (sue-DAN). The Kush had iron. They made tools and weapons with the iron. They were one of the first people to do so.

People from Egypt followed roads along the Nile River. They passed through the Kush lands. They carried ivory, ebony, and furs. The traders paid the Kush fees to use the roads. The Kush became rich.

Then, the Aksum kingdom came into power. The Aksum people were in charge of the routes. They traded crops, gold, and ivory on the coast of the Red Sea. Most merchants, or traders, going to the East went through the port of Aksum. It was on the Red Sea. This gave the Aksum rulers ties to India, Egypt, and the Roman Empire. It made them rich. Then, Arabs took over these trade routes. The Aksum people lost their power.

117

The Empire of Ghana

Muhammad (moo-HAM-uhd) was a religious man. He began a faith called Islam (is-LAWM). His followers are called Muslims (MUHZ-luhmz). Muslim traders went from North Africa to West Africa. They went through the Empire of Ghana (GAW-nuh). Ghana owned the main trade routes in northwest Africa.

The West Africans needed to keep their food from going bad. Adding salt to food made it safe to eat. It would not rot. The West Africans did not have salt. They had gold mines. So, the Muslims traded salt for their gold. Most of the world's gold came from West Africa.

At one point, the Muslims tried to force the people in Ghana to change faiths. There were fights. Then, the North Africans attacked. The Mali Empire took over the trade routes.

The Mali and Songhai Empires

The Mali rulers did not fight against the Muslims. They changed to Islam. This made the salt-gold trade work better than ever. Still, the empire had ended by the 1400s.

Next came the Songhai (son-GAH-ee) Empire. It had lots of soldiers. This empire stayed strong for 100 years. Then, the Moroccan (muh-RAW-kuhn) army came. They took over the gold mines of West Africa.

Swahili Culture

Traders sailed across the Indian Ocean. This ocean is located between Africa and Asia. The east coast had ports. Ships came in. Africans sold gold, shells, furs, ivory, and slaves. They bought goods, too. Many Arab Muslims visited these ports. Later, some of them made their homes there. Islam and the Arab language became a part of the culture. It is called Swahili (swaw-HEE-lee).

Comprehension Question

Why did the West Africans want salt?

African History

Africa is very large. It is the second largest continent in the world. It is larger than the United States and Europe put together. Africa lies south of Europe and southwest of the Middle East.

Trading goods made African cultures rich. As groups took charge of trade routes (paths), their power grew. When they lost control of these routes, they lost their power.

The Kush and the Kingdom of Aksum

The Kush (KUHSH) had one of the first civilizations (siv-uh-luh-ZAY-shuhnz) in Africa. They ruled what is now Sudan (sue-DAN). They were one of the first people to make iron tools. Egyptian (ee-JIP-shun) trade routes followed the Nile River. They passed through the Kush lands. People carried ivory, ebony, and furs on these paths. Since the Kush owned the roads, they charged a fee to use them. The Kush grew rich.

Then, the Aksum kingdom came into power. The Aksum people took charge of the trade routes. They traded crops, gold, and ivory along the Red Sea's coast. Most merchants, or traders, going to the East passed through Aksum's port city. It was on the Red Sea. This gave the Aksum rulers a tie to India, Egypt, and the Roman Empire. It brought them riches. Around A.D. 700, Arabs took over these trading routes. The Aksum people lost their power.

119

The Empire of Ghana

The prophet Muhammad (moo-HAM-uhd) began a faith called Islam (is-LAWM). His followers are called Muslims (MUHZ-luhmz). In the 700s, Muslim traders went from North Africa to West Africa. They moved through the Empire of Ghana (GAW-nuh). The West Africans needed a way to keep their food from going bad. Adding salt to food made it safe to eat. It would not rot. The West Africans did not have salt. But they did have gold. So, the Muslims traded salt for their gold. Most of the world's gold came from West Africa.

Ghana owned the main trade routes in northwest Africa. At one point, the Muslims tried to force the people of Ghana to change religions. The fighting made the empire weaker. Then, North Africans attacked Ghana. They took over the trade routes.

The Mali and Songhai Empires

The Mali also rose to power by owning trade routes. The Mali rulers did not fight with the Muslims. They switched to Islam. This made the salt-gold trade more successful than before. Still, the Mali Empire ended by the 1400s.

Next came the Songhai (son-GAH-ee) Empire. It grew more powerful than the Mali Empire. It stayed strong for 100 years. Then, the Moroccan (muh-RAW-kuhn) army ended it in 1591. They took over West Africa's gold mines.

Swahili Culture

Traders sailed the Indian Ocean. It lies between Africa and Asia. Africa had ports on its east coast. There, Africans sold gold, shells, furs, ivory, and slaves. They bought goods from Asia, Persia, and India. Many Arab Muslim merchants visited the ports on the African coast. In time, some of them made their homes there. The Arab language and Islam became a part of the culture. It is called Swahili (swaw-HEE-lee).

Comprehension Question

Why was salt important to the West Africans?

#50083 — *Leveled Texts: World Cultures*

African History

Africa is the second largest continent. It is bigger than the United States and Europe combined. Africa lies south of Europe and southwest of the Middle East.

Trading goods made the African cultures rich. When empires gained control of trade routes (paths), their power grew. When they lost control of these routes, they lost their power and wealth.

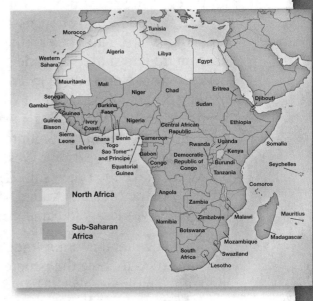

The Kush and the Kingdom of Aksum

The Kush (KUHSH) had one of the first civilizations (siv-uh-luh-ZAY-shuhnz) in Africa, ruling what is now the country of Sudan (sue-DAN). They made tools and weapons of iron. Egyptian (ee-JIP-shun) trade routes passed through the Kush kingdom. People carried ivory, ebony, and animal furs on these routes. Since the Kush owned these routes, they charged fees to use them. The Kush became rich.

The kingdom of Aksum rose to power in the first century A.D. The Aksum people traded crops, gold, and ivory along the coast of the Red Sea. Merchants going to the East passed through Aksum's port city on the Red Sea. This gave the Aksum rulers a connection to India, Egypt, and the Roman Empire and brought them great wealth. Around A.D. 700, Arabs took control of all these trading routes. The Aksum people lost their power.

The Empire of Ghana

The prophet Muhammad (moo-HAM-uhd) began the religion of Islam (is-LAWM) around A.D. 600. His followers are called Muslims (MUHZ-luhmz). In the 700s, Muslim traders started to trade gold. They traveled from North Africa to West Africa by moving through the Empire of Ghana (GAW-nuh). West Africans needed a way to keep their food from spoiling. Salt preserved food and made it safe to eat, but West Africans could not make their own salt. They had gold mines. So, the Muslims traded salt for gold. Most of the world's gold came from West Africa.

Ghana owned the major trade routes in northwest Africa. At one point, the Muslims tried to force the people of Ghana to change religions. The fighting made the empire weaker. Then, North Africans attacked Ghana and seized the trade routes. By 1203, Ghana had been taken over.

The Mali and Songhai Empires

The Mali also gained power by owning trade routes. The Mali leaders did not oppose the Muslims and converted to Islam. This made the salt-gold trade more successful than ever before. Still, the Mali Empire had ended by the 1400s.

Next came the Songhai (son-GAH-ee) Empire. It grew more powerful than the Mali Empire. It remained strong for 100 years. Then, the Moroccan (muh-RAW-kuhn) army ended it in 1591. They took over West Africa's gold mines.

Swahili Culture

Merchants sailed the Indian Ocean, which lies between Africa and Asia. Africa had seaports along its eastern coast. There, Africans sold gold, shells, animal skins, ivory, and slaves. They bought goods from Asia, Persia, and India. Many Arab Muslim merchants visited these ports on the African coast. In time, many of them owned homes in these ports. The Arab language and Islam became a part of the coastal culture called Swahili (swaw-HEE-lee).

Comprehension Question

Explain why the salt trade was important to West Africa.

122

African History

As the second largest continent, Africa is bigger than the entire United States and Europe put together. Africa lies south of Europe and southwest of the Middle East.

Ancient Africans grew wealthy from gold, ivory, and other trade goods. Different societies owned trade routes and charged fees to use them. Merchants needed these roadways to trade with other nations, which made the owners of trade routes very powerful. When empires gained control over trade routes, their power and wealth increased dramatically. When they lost control of these routes, they lost everything.

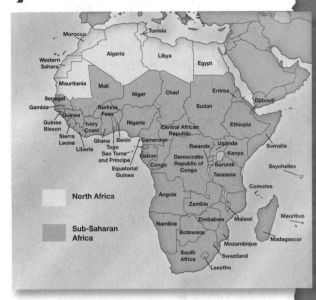

The Kush and the Kingdom of Aksum

The Kush (KUHSH) had one of the first civilizations (siv-uh-luh-ZAY-shuhnz) in Africa. They were one of the first peoples to work extensively with iron, crafting both tools and weapons. The Kush ruled what is now the country of Sudan (sue-DAN). Merchants carried ivory, ebony, and animal furs along the Nile River on the Egyptian (ee-JIP-shun) trade routes that passed through the Kush kingdom. The Kush grew wealthy from the fees they charged for the use of the roads.

The kingdom of Aksum rose to power in the first century A.D. when they traded crops, gold, and ivory along the coast of the Red Sea. Merchants traveling to the East passed through Aksum's port city on the Red Sea, providing Aksum rulers with connections to India, Egypt, and the Roman Empire. This civilization accumulated great wealth. However, around A.D. 700, Arabs seized control of the trading routes in the region, and the kingdom of Aksum disintegrated.

123

The Empire of Ghana

The prophet Muhammad (moo-HAM-uhd) started the religion of Islam (is-LAWM) around A.D. 600. His followers are Muslims (MUHZ-luhmz). In the 700s, Muslim merchants traveled from North Africa to West Africa by passing through the Empire of Ghana (GAW-nuh). West Africans needed a way to keep their food from spoiling. Salt preserved food and made it safe to eat, but West Africans had no salt. They had gold mines. So, the Muslims traded salt for gold. Most of the world's gold came from West Africa.

The Empire of Ghana controlled the major trade routes in northwest Africa. Then, the Muslims tried to force the people of Ghana to convert to Islam. The fighting weakened the empire. As a result, North Africans attacked and seized the trade routes. By 1203, Ghana had been taken over.

The Mali and Songhai Empires

The Mali leaders did not oppose the Muslims and they converted to Islam. This made the salt-gold trade more successful than ever before. Still, the Mali Empire ended by the 1400s.

Next came the Songhai (son-GAH-ee) Empire. With its great army, it grew even stronger than the Mali Empire had been. The Songhai remained powerful for 100 years until 1591, when the fierce Moroccan (muh-RAW-kuhn) military destroyed the empire. After that, the Moroccans had control of West Africa's gold mines.

Swahili Culture

Merchants sailed across the Indian Ocean between Africa and Asia. At seaports along Africa's eastern coast, the Africans bought imported goods from Asia, Persia, and India. They sold gold, shells, animal skins, ivory, and slaves. Many Arab Muslim merchants visited these ports. Some of them chose to live in these cities. As a result, the Arab language and Islam became a part of the coastal culture called Swahili (swaw-HEE-lee).

Comprehension Question

How did trading affect life in West Africa?

124

Mesoamerican Empires

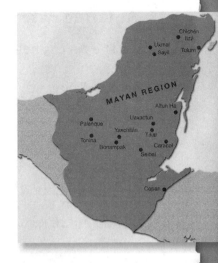

Mesoamerica is another name for Central America. It is a long piece of land. It joins North America to South America. Long ago, two American Indian tribes ruled here. They were the Mayas and the Aztecs.

Magnificent Mayas

The Mayas lived on the Yucatán Peninsula (yoo-kuh-TAN puhn-IN-suh-luh). They were farmers. They grew corn and squash. They put fertilizer (FUHR-tuhl-iz-uhr) into the dirt. It made their crops grow better. They grew their crops in fields on hills. These fields were called terraces (TAIR-ruhs-es). The terraces looked like huge steps going up the hills.

The Mayas had writing. They made a calendar. They did math. They built 100 cities using blocks of stone. They did this with no metal tools! Each city had its own king. They often fought against each other.

The Mayas honored the gods of nature. They built temples for the gods of rain and corn. Most cities had lots of temples. Some temples were 10 stories tall. The highest level was the smallest. Steps led to the top.

No one knows what happened to the Mayan civilization (siv-uh-luh-ZAY-shuhn). About 1,000 years ago, the Mayas left their cities. Perhaps they were killed by a sickness. Yet, some people in Central America today can trace their families back to the Mayas. These people are called descendents (dih-SEN-duhntz).

125

Amazing Aztecs

The Aztecs believed in many gods. Around 1325, the Aztec sun god told his people to move. They did not know where to go. The sun god said he would lead them. He said he would give them a sign. They should settle where they saw an eagle sitting on a cactus with a snake. They found this place. It was on an island. It was in the middle of a lake in central Mexico. They named it Tenochtitlan (tay-noch-teet-LAWN).

They built canals and used canoes. This let them move around the city. They built high roads. These roads joined the city to the mainland. When they had wars, they destroyed these roads. Then their enemies needed boats to attack.

The Aztecs had a legend. The legend told of a god named Quetzalcoatl (ket-sawl-kuh-WAH-tl). This god made the world. Then he made humans. He taught them how to farm. Quetzalcoatl left the Aztecs. He had to solve problems among the lower gods. But Quetzalcoatl said he would come back.

In 1502, the Aztec leader was Moctezuma II. He made people follow the rules. He even punished members of his own house who broke the law. Back then, kings were called weak if they showed mercy. Moctezuma was strong.

The Spanish came in the year that Quetzalcoatl was going to return. Moctezuma thought the Spanish leader might be the god. He let the Spanish into his city. He hoped to learn more about them. But after they arrived, the Spanish took him prisoner!

After a few months, the Aztecs rioted. The crowd yelled. They threw things. The Spanish brought out Moctezuma. They told him to calm his people. Instead, the Aztecs threw rocks at him. He died. Then, the Spanish stopped the rioting. They took charge. The Aztec empire ended.

Comprehension Question

Describe life for either the Mayas or the Aztecs.

126

Mesoamerican Empires

Mesoamerica is another name for Central America. This piece of land joins the continents of North America and South America. Long ago, two American Indian tribes ruled this area. They were the Mayas and the Aztecs.

Magnificent Mayas

The Mayas lived on the Yucatán Peninsula (yoo-kuh-TAN puhn-IN-suh-luh). They were farmers. They grew corn, squash, and cotton. They knew how to add fertilizer (FUHR-tuhl-iz-uhr) to dirt. They used terraces (TAIR-ruhs-es) to grow crops on hills. A terrace is a set of fields that looks like huge steps.

The Mayas had a form of writing. They made a calendar. They knew math. They understood the planets. They built more than 100 cities using blocks of stone. They did it without any metal tools! Each city-state had its own king. These kings often fought with one another.

The Mayas worshipped the gods of nature. They had temples to honor the rain and corn gods. Most cities had even more temples. Some towered 10 stories high. Like pyramids, the highest level was the smallest. They had steps that led to the top.

No one knows what happened to the Mayas. About 1,000 years ago, the Mayas left their cities. Yet, some people in Central America today can trace their families back to the Mayas. These people are called descendents (dih-SEN-duhntz).

Amazing Aztecs

Around 1325, a group called the Aztecs decided to move. They did not know where they were going. Their sun god said he would lead them to land. He told them to settle where they saw an eagle sitting on a cactus with a snake. They found this scene. It was on an island. It was right in the middle of a lake in central Mexico. They named it Tenochtitlan (tay-noch-teet-LAWN).

To get around the city, they built canals and used canoes. They built raised roads to join the city to the mainland. If war threatened, they wrecked these roads. Then, their enemies had to use boats to reach them.

The Aztecs thought that a god named Quetzalcoatl (ket-sawl-kuh-WAH-tl) made the world. Then, he formed humans. He taught them how to farm. Quetzalcoatl left the Aztecs. He had to go solve problems among the lower gods. But, he said he would come back.

In 1502, the Aztec leader was Moctezuma II. He made everyone follow the rules. He even punished members of his own house who broke the law. Back then, kings were called weak if they showed mercy. Moctezuma was strong.

The Spanish came in the year of Quetzalcoatl's expected return. Moctezuma thought the Spanish leader might be Quetzalcoatl. He let the Spanish into his city. He hoped to learn more about them. But after they arrived, the Spanish took him prisoner!

After a few months, the Aztecs rioted. The crowd yelled and threw things. The Spanish brought out Moctezuma. They told him to calm his people. Instead, the Aztecs stoned him to death. The Spanish stopped the rioters. The Aztec empire had ended.

Comprehension Question

Describe life for the Mayas and the Aztecs.

#50083— *Leveled Texts: World Cultures*   © *Shell Education*

Mesoamerican Empires

Mesoamerica is another name for Central America. This piece of land joins the North American and South American continents. Long ago, two American Indian tribes ruled this area. They were the Mayas and the Aztecs.

Magnificent Mayas

Mayan kings ruled city-states located on the Yucatán Peninsula (yoo-kuh-TAN puhn-IN-suh-luh). The Mayas were great farmers and were one of the first people to add fertilizer (FUHR-tuhl-iz-uhr) to soil. They used terraces (TAIR-ruhs-es) to grow corn, squash, and cotton on hillsides. A terrace is like a series of huge steps.

The Mayas had a form of writing and a calendar. They understood math. They knew about the movement of the planets. They built more than 100 cities using blocks of stone. Mayan engineers built without metal tools. Each city-state had its own king. These kings often fought with one another.

Since farming was so important, the Mayas worshipped the gods of nature. Temples honored the rain and corn gods. Most cities had even more temples. Some towered 10 stories high. Like pyramids, the highest level was the smallest. Steps on the outside of the temples led to the top.

No one is sure exactly what happened to the great Mayan civilization (siv-uh-luh-ZAY-shuhn). About 1,000 years ago, the Mayas abandoned their cities. Yet, their descendents (dih-SEN-duhntz) still live in Central America. They can trace their families back to the Mayas.

129

Amazing Aztecs

Around 1325, a group called the Aztecs decided to move. They did not know where they were going, but their sun god promised to give them a sign. He said they should live where they saw an eagle sitting on a cactus with a snake. They found this scene on an island right in the middle of a lake in central Mexico. They named it Tenochtitlan (tay-noch-teet-LAWN).

To get around the city, they built canals and used canoes. They built highways stretching across the lake to the mainland. If war threatened, they destroyed these highways so that their enemies could not reach them without boats.

The Aztec god Quetzalcoatl (ket-sawl-kuh-WAH-tl) was most important. Myths tell how he created the world, formed humans, and helped them grow corn. Because he had to solve problems among the gods, he had to leave the Aztecs. But, Quetzalcoatl promised he would return to them one day.

In 1502, the leader Moctezuma II was chosen. As the new leader, Moctezuma strictly enforced rules. He even harshly punished members of his own house who broke the law. Back then, kings were considered weak if they showed compassion. Moctezuma was strong.

By coincidence, the Spanish arrived in the year of Quetzalcoatl's expected return. Moctezuma thought the Spanish leader might be Quetzalcoatl. Moctezuma let the Spanish enter his capital. He hoped to learn more about them. But shortly after they arrived, the Spanish took him prisoner! After a few months, the Aztecs grew restless and began rioting. The Spanish brought out Moctezuma to calm his people, but the Aztecs stoned him to death. The Spanish stopped the rioting, took charge, and ended the Aztec empire.

Comprehension Question

Compare and contrast the Aztecs
and Mayas.

Mesoamerican Empires

Mesoamerica is another name for Central America, the land that joins the continents of North America and South America. Long ago, the Mayas and the Aztecs, two advanced American Indian tribes, ruled this region.

Magnificent Mayas

The Mayas lived on the Yucatán Peninsula (yoo-kuh-TAN puhn-IN-suh-luh). As skillful farmers, they were one of the first people to add fertilizer (FUHR-tuhl-iz-uhr) to soil to enhance their crops. They used terraces (TAIR-ruhs-es) to grow corn, squash, and cotton on mountainsides. Terraces were fields that looked like a series of huge steps.

The Mayas developed a system of writing and a calendar. They understood math and the movement of the planets. They built more than 100 cities using gigantic blocks of stone—an amazing achievement since they had no metal tools. A different king ruled each city-state and these kings often fought with one another.

Since farming was so important, the Mayas worshipped the gods of nature. Each city had temples honoring the rain and corn gods. Most cities had even more temples. Some towered 10 stories high. Steps on the outside of these structures led to the top, and like pyramids, the highest level was the smallest.

Nobody is certain exactly what happened to the Mayan civilization (siv-uh-luh-ZAY-shuhn). Around 1,000 years ago, the Mayas abandoned their cities. Perhaps a deadly disease killed the majority of them. Yet their descendents (dih-SEN-duhntz) still live in Central America and can trace their families back to Mayan ancestors.

#50083—Leveled Texts: World Cultures

Amazing Aztecs

Around 1325, the sun god told the Aztecs to settle where they saw an eagle sitting on a cactus with a snake. They located this scene on an island in the middle of a lake in central Mexico. There they built the city of Tenochtitlan (tay-noch-teet-LAWN).

To get around the city, they built canals and used canoes. They built highways that stretched across the lake and connected Tenochtitlan to the mainland. When war threatened, they destroyed these highways so that their enemies needed boats to launch an attack against them.

The Aztec god Quetzalcoatl (ket-sawl-kuh-WAH-tl) was most important. A myth tells how he created the world, formed humans, and taught them to grow corn. Because he had to solve problems among the other gods, he had to leave the Aztecs. But, Quetzalcoatl promised he would return one day.

In 1502, the Aztec leader was Moctezuma II. Moctezuma so strictly enforced rules that he even harshly punished members of his own household who broke the law. Back then, kings were considered weak if they showed compassion, and Moctezuma was powerful.

By coincidence, the Spanish arrived in the year of Quetzalcoatl's expected return, so Moctezuma thought the Spanish leader might be Quetzalcoatl. Moctezuma let the Spanish enter Tenochtitlan in hopes of learning more about them. But shortly after they arrived, they took him prisoner! After a few months, the Aztecs grew restless and started rioting. The Spanish brought out Moctezuma to calm his people, but the Aztecs threw rocks, stoning him to death. Then, the Spanish stopped the rioting, seized control, and ended the mighty Aztec empire.

Comprehension Question

Would you have rather been an Aztec or a Maya?

#50083— *Leveled Texts: World Cultures*

The Incredible Incas

The Incas built an empire about 500 years ago. The empire was located in South America. It included the Andes (AN-deez) Mountains. Some Incas lived in the hills. Others lived in the valleys. Most of the towns were built in the valleys.

The Incas built thousands of miles of stone roads. These roads connected the six million Incas. Men ran along these roads to send news. In one day, relay teams could go hundreds of miles. But, it was hard to go through the mountains. So, the Incas built bridges. The bridges were held up by ropes.

Most Incas had homes made out of stucco (STUH-ko). Stucco is a thick mixture of sand and water. It is put on the outside of stone buildings. It gets hard as it dries.

Some farmers lived in the mountains. They used terraces (TAIR-ruhs-es) to plant potatoes and corn. The terraces were fields. They looked like a set of huge steps. The cool, dry climate let the people store their food for later use. They did not go hungry.

The Incas had no money. They traded with each other for the things they needed. They did not write. But they did keep track of things. They used knots on strings. A set of knotted strings made a *quipu* (KEY-poo). The *quipu* readers used the strings to record things. They recorded the amounts of crops and animals. They told how many people lived in a town. Each town had readers. Only they could read the strings.

The Incas made cloth from cotton and wool. Some people made things from gold and silver. Others were builders. They cut huge stones by hand. They built without mortar. Mortar is cement. It goes between bricks. The Incas placed the stones so perfectly that many of their buildings still stand. One city built by the Incas was Machu Picchu (MAW-choo PEE-choo). People have learned much about the Incas from this city.

#50083—Leveled Texts: World Cultures

Secrets from the Past

The Incas honored the gods of fire and thunder. Inti was the sun god. He made sure the crops grew. Priests made sacrifices (SAK-ruh-fice-ez) to please the gods. Sometimes they killed humans. They picked the most beautiful woman or strongest man. People felt important if chosen!

The Incas made mummies. When people died, they were wrapped in layers of cotton. In each layer, they put things that the person had owned. Some mummies had lots of things in their wraps. A few weighed more than half a ton! The dry air preserved the mummies. (Preserved means kept from rotting.) Some mummies still have skin, eyes, and nails.

ATHABALIBA
ultimus Rex Peruanorum.

Incan Leadership

A man called the Sapa Inca ruled the Incas. The Incas thought that the Sapa Inca was related to Inti. So, he was seen as a god.

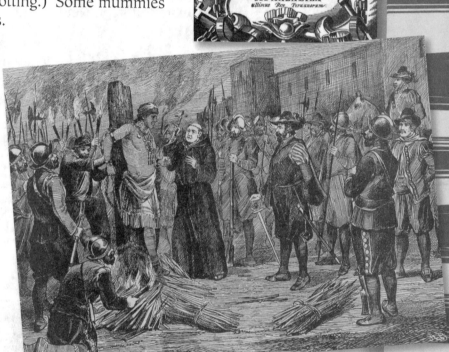

The Spanish came. They brought diseases with them. The Sapa Inca got sick and died. Then, his sons fought each other. Atahualpa (aw-tuh-WAWL-puh) won. He became the new Sapa Inca. But, this war made the Incas weak. The Spanish had the chance to take control.

When Francisco Pizarro (puh-ZAWR-oh) arrived in 1532, he caught Atahualpa. He killed him. Then the Spanish took charge. They ended the Incan Empire.

Comprehension Question

Describe the Incan Empire.

The Incredible Incas

About 500 years ago, the Incas built an empire. It was in South America. It included the Andes (AN-deez) Mountain chain. Some Incas lived in valley cities. Others lived in the mountains.

Fifteen thousand miles (24,140 km) of stone roads connected the six million Incas. Men carrying news ran along these roads. In just one day, relay teams could go 250 miles (402 km). To make it easier to move through the mountains, they built rope suspension (suh-SPEN-shuhn) bridges.

Most Incas lived in stucco (STUH-ko) homes. Stucco is a thick mixture of sand and water. It is put on the outside of stone buildings. It hardens as it dries. Some farmers lived in the mountains. They terraced the hillsides. The terraces (TAIR-ruhs-es) were potato and corn fields. They looked like a set of huge steps. The cool, dry climate let them store their food for future use. Hunger was never a problem.

The Incas did not have money. They traded with each other for the things they needed. They had no written language. They kept track of things using knots on strings. A set of knotted strings made up a quipu (KEY-poo). The quipu readers used the strings to record amounts of crops and animals. They told how many people lived in a town. Each town had readers. Only they could read the strings.

Many Incas were craftsmen. They made things from cotton, wool, gold, and silver. Others were builders. They cut huge stones by hand. They built without mortar. Mortar is the cement between bricks. They placed the stones so perfectly that many of their buildings still stand. One city was Machu Picchu (MAW-choo PEE-choo). No one has disturbed it. Its ruins are in great shape. People have learned much about the Incas from this city.

 #50083—Leveled Texts: World Cultures

Secrets from the Past

The Incas honored the gods of lightning, thunder, and mountains. Inti was the sun god. He made sure the crops grew. Priests offered sacrifices (SAK-ruh-fice-ez) to please the gods. Sometimes these were humans. They killed the most beautiful woman or strongest man. People felt honored to be chosen!

The Incas made mummies. They wrapped their dead in layers of cotton. In each layer, they put things that the person owned. Some mummies had lots of things inside their wraps. A few weighed more than half a ton! The dry air preserved the mummies. (Preserved means kept from decay.) Some mummies still have skin, eyes, and nails.

Incan Leadership

A man called the Sapa Inca ruled the Incas. The Incas thought that Inti was the Sapa Inca's ancestor. He was viewed as a god.

When the Spanish came, they brought diseases with them. The Sapa Inca died from one of these sicknesses. Then, his sons fought each other for control. Atahualpa (aw-tuh-WAWL-puh) won. He became the new Sapa Inca. But, their war had weakened the Incas. The Spanish had the chance to take control.

When Francisco Pizarro (puh-ZAWR-oh) arrived in 1532, he caught and killed Atahualpa. Then the Spanish took control. They ended the Incan Empire.

Comprehension Question

What was the most important part of the Incan Empire?

#50083 — *Leveled Texts: World Cultures*

The Incredible Incas

About 500 years ago, the Incas built an empire in South America. It included the Andes (AN-deez) Mountain chain. Some Incas lived in valley cities while others lived in the mountains.

Fifteen thousand miles (24,140 km) of stone roads connected the six million Incas living in the empire. Messengers carrying news ran along these roads. In just one day, relay teams could cover 250 miles (402 km). To make it easier to move through the mountains, they built rope suspension (suh-SPEN-shuhn) bridges.

Most Incas lived in stucco (STUH-ko) homes. Stucco is a thick mixture of sand and water that hardens as it dries on the outside of stone buildings. Farmers living in the mountains terraced the mountainsides. These terraces (TAIR-ruhs-es) were fields of potatoes and corn that looked like a series of huge steps. The cool, dry climate allowed them to freeze-dry their food and safely store it for future use. Hunger was never a problem.

The Incas did not have money. They traded with each other for the things they needed. They had no written language, either, but they kept track of things using a system of knots on strings. The knotted strings made up a quipu (KEY-poo). The quipu readers used the strings to keep track of amounts of crops and animals. They also told how many people lived in a town and who was married. Each village had readers who were the only ones who could understand the messages.

The Incas were craftsmen who made things from cotton, wool, gold, and silver. They were skilled builders. They cut huge stones by hand and built things without mortar. Mortar is the cement between bricks. They placed the stones so perfectly that some of their buildings still stand. Many are in the city of Machu Picchu (MAW-choo PEE-choo). No one has disturbed Machu Picchu, so its ruins are in excellent shape. Archaeologists have learned much about the Incas from this city.

© Shell Education　　　　　　#50083—Leveled Texts: World Cultures

Secrets from the Past

The Incas worshipped the gods of nature. They honored the gods of lightning, thunder, and mountains. Inti, the sun god, controlled the success of their crops. To please the gods, priests offered sacrifices (SAK-ruh-fice-ez). Sometimes these sacrifices were human. They killed the most beautiful woman or the strongest man. People felt honored to be chosen!

The Incas made mummies by wrapping their dead in many layers of cotton. In each layer, they placed items that had belonged to the person. Some of these mummies had so many items in their wraps that they weighed more than half a ton! The dry air preserved the mummies. Even now some still have skin, eyes, and fingernails.

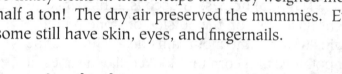

ATHABALIBA

Incan Leadership

A man called the Sapa Inca ruled the Incas. The Incas thought that the Sapa Inca was Inti's descendent.

When the Spanish came to Peru, they brought European diseases with them. One of these sicknesses killed the Sapa Inca. Then, his sons fought each other for control. Atahualpa (aw-tuh-WAWL-puh) won and became the new Sapa Inca. But, their war had weakened the Incas and given the Spanish the opportunity to seize land.

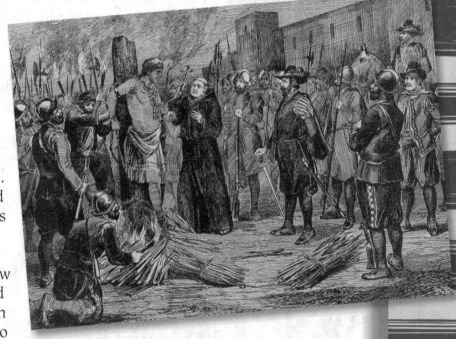

When the Spanish explorer Francisco Pizarro (puh-ZAWR-oh) arrived in 1532, he easily caught and killed Atahualpa. Then, the Spanish took control and ended the Incan Empire.

Comprehension Question

Why is it important to learn about the Incas?

#50083 — *Leveled Texts: World Cultures*

The Incredible Incas

About 500 years ago, the Incas built an empire in South America that included the Andes (AN-deez) Mountain chain. Some Incas lived in valley cities while others lived in the mountains.

Fifteen thousand miles (24,140 km) of stone roads connected the Incan population of six million. Messengers carrying news ran along these roads. In just one day, relay teams could cover 250 miles (402 km). To make it easier to travel through the mountains, they installed rope suspension (suh-SPEN-shuhn) bridges.

Most Incas lived in stucco (STUH-ko) homes. Stucco is a thick mixture of sand and water that hardens as it dries on the outside of stone buildings. Farmers terraced the mountainsides. These terraces (TAIR-ruhs-es) were fields of potatoes and corn that looked like a series of gigantic steps. The cool, dry climate allowed the people to freeze-dry their food and safely store it for future use, so starvation was never a problem.

Many Incan artisans fashioned things using cotton, wool, gold and silver. Others were skilled builders who cut stones by hand and built things without using mortar. Mortar is the cement between bricks. They placed the stones so perfectly that many of their buildings still stand. One important city was Machu Picchu (MAW-choo PEE-choo). Nobody ever disturbed Machu Picchu, so its ruins are in excellent condition, and archaeologists have discovered much about the Incas from this city.

The Incas did not have money, so they traded with each other for the things they needed. They had no written language, either, but they kept track of things with a system of knots on strings. The knotted strings made up a quipu (KEY-poo). The quipu readers used the strings to keep track of amounts of crops and animals. They also told how many people lived in a town and who was married. Each village had quipu readers who were the only ones who could understand the messages.

© Shell Education   #50083—Leveled Texts: World Cultures

Secrets from the Past

The Incas worshipped the gods of nature, including the gods of lightning, thunder, and mountains. Inti, the sun god, controlled the success of their crops. To please the gods, priests offered sacrifices (SAK-ruh-fice-ez), and sometimes these sacrifices were human. They killed the most beautiful woman or the strongest man. People felt honored to be selected!

The Incas made mummies by wrapping their corpses in many layers of cotton. Inside each layer, they placed objects that had belonged to the person. Some of these mummies had so many things within their wraps that they ended up weighing more than half a ton! The dry air preserved the mummies so well that even now some of them have skin, eyes, and fingernails.

Incan Leadership

A man called the Sapa Inca ruled the Incas. The Incas believed that the Sapa Inca was Inti's descendent and worshipped him as divine.

When the Spanish arrived in Peru, they brought European diseases with them. The Sapa Inca perished from one of these sicknesses. Then his sons battled for control. Atahualpa (aw-tuh-WAWL-puh) won and became the new Sapa Inca. However, their war had weakened the Incas and given the Spanish the opportunity to seize land.

When the Spanish explorer Francisco Pizarro (puh-ZAWR-oh) came in 1532, he easily captured and killed Atahualpa. Then, the Spanish took control and ended the Incan Empire.

Comprehension Question

What do people today learn by studying the Incas?

Resources

Works Cited

August, Diane and Timothy Shanahan (Eds). (2006). *Developing literacy in second-language learners: Report of the National Literacy Panel on language-minority children and youth.* Mahwah, NJ: Lawrence Erlbaum Associates, Inc.

Marzano, Robert, Debra Pickering, and Jane Pollock. (2001). *Classroom instruction that works.* Alexandria, VA: Association for Supervision and Curriculum Development.

Tomlinson, Carol Ann. (2000). Leadership for Differentiating Schools and Classrooms, Alexandria, VA: Association for Supervision and Curriculum Development.

Image Sources

Page	Description	Photo Credit/Source	Filename
21, 23, 25, 27, (top)	Map of Mesopotamia	Teacher Created Materials	mesomap.jpg
21, 23, 25, 27, (bottom)	Cuneiform tablets	B. Speckart/Shutterstock, Inc. (969736)	cuneifrm.jpg
22, 24, 26, 28	Ziggurat	The Library of Congress, Prints and Photographs Division. Washington, D.C. (LC-M33-14467)	ziggurat.jpg
29, 31, 33, 35	Map of Hebrew land	Teacher Created Materials	hebrwmap.jpg
30, 32, 34, 36, (top)	Assyria—Portal Guardian from Nimroud	The Library of Congress, Prints and Photographs Division. Washington, D.C. (LC-DIG-ppmsca-04982)	assyria.jpg
30, 32, 34, 36, (bottom)	Phoenician alphabet	Teacher Created Materials	alphabt1.jpg
37, 39, 41, 43	Map of Egypt	Teacher Created Materials	egptmap1.jpg
38, 40, 42, 44, (top)	Egyptian casket	Scott Rothstein/Shutterstock, Inc. (1531518)	casket.jpg
38, 40, 42, 44, (bottom)	Mummy	Scott Rothstein/Shutterstock, Inc. (1533285)	mummy.jpg
45, 47, 49, 51, (top)	Map of Egypt	The Library of Congress, Prints and Photographs Division. Washington, D.C. http://hdl.loc.gov/loc.gmd/g7420.ct000420	egptmap2.jpg
45, 47, 49, 51, (bottom)	Ramses II's temple Abu Simbel	Vladimir Pomortzeff/ Shutterstock, Inc. (873170)	ramses.jpg
46, 48, 50, 52, (top)	Tutankhamun's mask	Courtesy of Corinne Burton	mask.jpg
46, 48, 50, 52, (bottom)	Alexander the Great	Vladimir Korostyshevskiy/ Shutterstock, Inc. (556983)	alex.jpg
53, 55, 57, 59, (top)	Grecian urn	David Shawley/Shutterstock, Inc. (116496)	urn.jpg

Resources (cont.)

Image Sources (cont.)

Page	Description	Photo Credit/Source	Filename
53, 55, 57, 59, (bottom)	Ancient Greek theater	Roman Milert/Shutterstock, Inc. (934787)	theater.jpg
54, 56, 58, 60, (top)	Bust of Homer	Barry G. Hurt/Shutterstock, Inc. (664282)	homer.jpg
54, 56, 58, 60, (bottom)	Aristotle	Dhoxax/Shutterstock, Inc. (271618)	aristotl.jpg
61, 63, 65, 67	Greek alphabet	Teacher Created Materials	alphabt2.jpg
62, 64, 66, 68	Acropolis of Athens	Nick Koumaris/Shutterstock, Inc. (1157568)	acropols.jpg
69, 71, 73, 75, (top)	Trajan's forum	Stephen Rudolph/Shutterstock, Inc. (1157568)	trajan.jpg
69, 71, 73, 75, (bottom)	Map of the campaigns of Julius Caesar	Teacher Created Materials	caesrmap.jpg
70, 72, 74, 76, (top)	Julius Caesar	Heather L. Jones/Shutterstock, Inc. (566270)	caesar.jpg
70, 72, 74, 76, (bottom)	Carvings of women	Corel (Turkey CD Volume II 47113)	carvings.jpg
77, 79, 81, 83, (top)	Minerva	Zastavkin/Shutterstock, Inc. (83292)	minerva.jpg
77, 79, 81, 83, (bottom)	Vatican City	Corel (Rome CD 149046)	vatican.jpg
78, 80, 82, 84, (top)	Roman Catholic Church	Stanislav Khrapov/Shutterstock, Inc. (553911)	church.jpg
78, 80, 82, 84, (bottom)	Trajan's market	Corel (Rome CD 149022)	market.jpg
85, 87, 89, 91, (top)	Map of the Indus Valley	Teacher Created Materials	indusmap.jpg
85, 87, 89, 91, (bottom)	Dravidian architecture	Corel (India CD 71008)	dravdian.jpg
86, 88, 90, 92, (top)	Map of Ashoka's Empire	Teacher Created Materials	ashoka.jpg
86, 88, 90, 92, (bottom)	Buddha meditating	Public Domain: http://commons.wikimedia.org/wiki/Image:Buddha-Sarnath-sepia.jpg	buddha1.jpg
93, 95, 97, 99, (top)	Map of Gupta Empire	Teacher Created Materials	guptamap.jpg
93, 95, 97, 99, (bottom)	Taj Mahal	Kharidehal Abhirama Ashwin/Shutterstock, Inc. (1476907)	tajmahal.jpg
94, 96, 98, 100	Gandhi	The Library of Congress, Prints and Photographs Division. Washington, D.C. (LC-USZ62-97294)	gandhi.jpg
101, 103, 105, 107	Great Wall of China	WizData, Inc./Shutterstock, Inc. (937085)	greatwal.jpg